Award Wi

ROCKSON RAPU

Pioneering Campaign for
Biofuels as Alternative Energy
Solution

OIL TO FUNCTION

First Edition Published by
Copyright © 2024
WOW Book Publishing™
All rights reserved. Neither this book, nor any parts within it may be sold or reproduced in any form without permission.
No part of this book may be reproduced in any form or by any electronic or mechanical means including information storage, retrieval systems, audios, videos and movies without permission in writing from the author. The only exception is by a reviewer, who may quote short excerpts in a review.
The views and opinions expressed in this book are that of the author based on his personal experiences and education. The author does not guarantee that anyone following the techniques, suggestions, ideas, or strategies in this book will become successful. The author shall neither be liable nor responsible for any loss or damage allegedly arising from any information or suggestion in this book.
ISBN: 9798320263335

DEDICATION

This book is dedicated to my team at Refined Group, including my beautiful and diligent children, who have been incredibly supportive throughout this project, enabling me to initiate a campaign of this magnitude.

THANK YOU

This is just to say thank you for buying my book. Please endeavour to visit our website to download some free resource materials that will help you impact lives. Also follow me on Facebook, Instagram @rocksonrapu and subscribe to our YouTube channel.

Visit our website:
http://www.refinedresources.co.uk

OIL TO FUNCTION

CONTENTS

	Acknowledgments	1
	Preface	2
1	The Prophetic Campaign Journey	6
2	The Oil Landscape of Nigeria	11
3	Oils With Potential: A Comparative Analysis	31
4	Case Studies of Success	45
5	Palm Oil: The Golden Crop	54
6	Biofuel Revolution: Palm Oil in Automobiles	69
7	The Green Advantage	84
8	From Local to Global	100
9	The Socio-Economic Ripple Effect	117
10	The Future of Oil	130
11	Market Dynamics and Trends	136
12	Policy and Regulation Forecast	140
13	Cultural Shifts and Consumer Behaviour	144
14	Scenarios for Sustainable Growth	147

Further Reading	151
About the Author	154

ACKNOWLEDGMENTS

I thank our Lord God for blessing me with the best resources to write this book. I am especially thankful to Him for the gift of story-telling, which has enabled me to simplify what others had mystified, by adopting an approach that intertwines cultural storytelling with modern campaign techniques.

I thank God for all the crusaders and researchers for their efforts towards renewable energy. I am highly privileged to transform their stories into a book that could ginger Nigeria and Africa to massively invest in this area.

I appreciate the prayers of my brothers, sisters, Pastors, Bishops and Apostles who have been standing in the gap for me.

I want to honour few friends, relatives, and mentors for their invaluable support: Vishal Morjaria, Nosa Eweka, Emmanuel Egerton-Shyngle, Dr Tony Rapu, Pastor Sunny Odafe, Apostle Alph Lukau and Bishop Celeste Lukau and many more that I do not have enough space to mention here.

PREFACE

Motivation from Oil Spillage

Once upon a time, in the heart of Nigeria's Niger Delta region, a young and ambitious graduate named Rockson Rapu, embarked on his first-ever job at the esteemed oil company, NNPC - Nigerian National Petroleum Corporation. In those days, it was prestigious to work in NNPC at any level.

Fresh out of university, and armed with a degree in Biochemistry, Rockson Rapu was determined to make a difference in the face of the devastating oil spills that had long plagued the delicate ecosystem.

The Hand of God was upon the young lad, so that from his first day on the job, he saw the big picture and quickly realized the magnitude of the challenge that lay before him. The Niger Delta, known in time past for its lush mangroves, biodiversity in flora and fauna, and crystal-clear waterways, had been suffering under the weight of decades of oil exploration and extraction. The picturesque landscape had now become marred by countless oil spills, leaving a devastating impact on the environment and the local communities who depended on it for their livelihood.

It did not take him time to settle down at NNPC Port Harcourt where by the grace of God, he was quickly assigned as team leader to a group of NYSC microbiologists and biochemists in a department headed by Dr. Idoniboye. They analyzed samples from oil spill zones around the Niger Delta. It was a good learning curve for the young man who loved research work. Above his manager Dr. Idoniboye were other big bosses including Dr Ibe and Dr. Isokriari.

This job meant that he was on the road most of the time. They were on the road with very rugged NNPC Land Rovers penetrating villages and getting samples from areas where oil had spilled and affected the livelihood of the villagers. Tour duties outside River State especially those extremely far away in Delta state, required them to use the small NNPC-hired aircrafts which they called Twin-Otters. This is a utility aircraft with the capacity for about 18 passengers. It was this aircraft which they flew many times that made him start thinking more about the environment and pollution

Determined to make a difference, Rockson Rapu dedicated long hours to studying the ecological ramifications of oil spills. He delved into research papers, engaged in informative discussions with experts, and even unofficially visited affected communities to understand their struggles first hand. Armed with knowledge and a deep sense of purpose, he began exploring the possibilities of replacing either partially or fully, the use of petrol, diesel, and engine oil in vehicles or other petrol consuming machines like petrol strimmers and power generators for electricity. This he believed would help to mitigate the impact of oil spills in our communities, and cut down the pollution in our towns and villages.

With a lot of information gathered over the past decades, he decided to launch this campaign to ginger the authorities and industrialists, to invest in alternative energy solutions in Nigeria. The campaign through this book will focus on the following:

- Mapping the Natural Oil Reserves in Nigeria, and looking at the geographical distribution of oil-bearing crops that stretch across the nation
- Identifying different kinds of oils that are naturally occurring and abundant in Nigeria and reviewing their present status and use and benefits to mankind as biofuels
- Selecting and analyzing the oils that have very high potentials for both local use and exports.

- Singling out few, including Palm Oil that are exceptionally useful with high added values and great potentials for replacing petrol, diesel and engine oil.

- Focusing on Palm oil alone as the winner of the few exceptionally useful oils with great added values and export potentials.

- Explaining how palm oil could be used for electricity generators and automobile, alongside petrol, diesel, and engine oil.

- Exploring the export potentials of Palm oil for use as alternative energy source in Africa, Middle East and South East Asia.

- Recognising that Africa, with its vast natural resources and abundant sunlight, has the potential to become a powerhouse of renewable energy. The continent has substantial natural oils, wind, solar, hydropower, and geothermal resources that, if properly harnessed, can partner with biofuels to provide electricity to millions, significantly reducing dependence on fossil fuels.

Chapter One

The Prophetic Campaign Journey

The Motivation

Rockson Rapu, with his first degree in Biochemistry, embarked on his professional journey at the Nigerian National Petroleum Corporation (NNPC) after completing his studies. His role as Team Leader for the NYSC scientists, involved the assessment of oil spill areas in the Niger Delta. Witnessing the devastating effects of pollution caused by oil spills fuelled Rockson Rapu's passion for finding alternative sources of energy. Consequently, he developed a firm determination to replace petrol and diesel, either fully or partially with plant or vegetable oils as a means to lessen the environmental impact of petroleum. This essay will explore Rockson Rapu's experiences, motivations, and initiatives as he spearheads the quest for sustainable energy solutions in Nigeria.

Working in the Niger Delta:

As Rockson Rapu stepped into the role of an NYSC scientist at NNPC, he was faced with the harsh reality of the ecological devastation caused by oil spills in the Niger Delta. Witnessing first-hand the contamination and destruction of wildlife habitats, the disruption of local communities, and the detrimental impacts on human health profoundly affected Rockson Rapu's perspective. He realized that the petroleum industry's reliance on fossil fuels came at a great cost to the environment and local communities alike.

Dreaming of Alternative Energy Sources:

Driven by his desire to mitigate the harmful effects of petroleum pollution, Rockson Rapu began to dream of replacing petrol and diesel with plant or vegetable oil as an alternative fuel source. Recognizing the need for sustainable energy, he envisioned a future where renewable fuels could power vehicles without causing such severe environmental damage. This dream became the catalyst for his subsequent actions and initiatives.

Leaving NNPC after Youth Service:

After gaining valuable experience and knowledge about the dire consequences of oil spills, Rockson Rapu eventually left his position at NNPC. Armed with determination, he resolved to devote his efforts to finding and promoting alternative energy sources that would reduce the negative impact of petroleum-related pollutants on the environment.

Advocating for Biofuels:

Upon leaving NNPC, Rockson Rapu redirected his focus towards the advancement of biofuels. Understanding that plant or vegetable oils could be converted into clean-burning, sustainable fuels, he began campaigning for wider adoption of these energy sources. Through research and partnerships, he initiated pilot projects to showcase the viability and environmental benefits of embracing biofuels, successfully raising awareness about their potential.

Collaborating with Stakeholders:

Realizing the significance of collaboration, Rockson Rapu actively sought out like-minded individuals and organizations to support his vision. He engaged with energy experts, scientists, and entrepreneurs, fostering partnerships that would aid in developing renewable energy solutions. By leveraging collective expertise and resources, Rockson Rapu aimed to accelerate progress in reducing Nigeria's dependence on petroleum-based fuels.

Addressing Challenges:

Rockson Rapu faced numerous challenges as he pursued his alternative energy goals. Limited financial resources, technological barriers, and resistance from established petroleum industries posed hurdles to his vision. However, he remained undeterred, employing innovation and perseverance to overcome obstacles and consistently move forward with local and foreign support.

Educating and Raising Awareness:

To garner support for his cause, Rockson Rapu actively engaged in educating industrialists and policymakers, both locally and abroad, about the environmental advantages of biofuels. He started organizing workshops, seminars, and awareness campaigns on social media, using his book to highlight the detrimental effects of petroleum on the environment and the potential for alternative energy sources to alleviate these problems. His efforts will hopefully help spark a national conversation about the need to transition to renewable energy using locally available natural oils. Through his book, Rockson Rapu plans to also engage the public to see how a change of mindset could help to promote the shift to biofuels.

Government and Policy Advocacy:

Recognizing the importance of government support, Rockson Rapu is now lobbying policymakers and decision-makers for the implementation of policies that would facilitate the adoption of biofuels in Nigeria. By demonstrating the potential economic and environmental benefits of embracing sustainable energy, he will persuade authorities to invest in research and development, provide incentives for renewable energy projects, and incentivise the transition away from fossil fuels.

The Aftermath:
Rockson Rapu's journey from working in the oil industry to becoming a champion for sustainable energy solutions in Nigeria exemplifies the potential for personal experiences to foster a deep commitment to positive change. His first-hand experience with the harmful impact of oil spills ignited a passion for finding alternative energy sources to reduce environmental pollution. Through his unwavering dedication, Rockson Rapu is spearheading the use of plant and vegetable oil as a biofuel, promoting its benefits, and advocating for its wider adoption. His efforts demonstrate that with dedication and determination, one can foster a national conversation and pave the way for a greener, more sustainable future.

Chapter Two

The Oil Landscape of Nigeria

Mapping the Oil Reserves - How It All Started

In the soft, golden light of dawn, the Nigerian landscape awakens to the songs of birds and the rustle of palm fronds swaying in the gentle breeze. This is a scene that has remained unchanged for centuries, a testament to the enduring bond between the land and its people. Yet, beneath this tranquil tableau lies a history forged through the fires of ambition, discovery, and the relentless pursuit of progress.

As we embark on this historical journey, let us travel back to a time when the first explorers set foot upon the rich soils of Nigeria, their hearts set on unearthing treasures that were whispered to lie beneath the verdant canopy. The discovery of crude oil in the late 1950s marked a pivotal moment, setting the stage for an era that would forever alter the landscape of Nigerian energy and economy.

Those nascent years of oil exploration were a harbinger of prosperity, transforming the nation into a burgeoning powerhouse within the global oil market. Yet, as the decades passed, a growing reliance on this 'black gold' cast a shadow over the nation, with economic ebbs and flows tethered to the whims of the world's oil appetite.

From past to present, we find ourselves at a crossroads, where the blessings of oil wealth have been tempered by the challenges of environmental concerns, volatile market dynamics, and the urgent call for sustainable alternatives. The very history that once fueled our ascent now whispers of change, urging us to look beyond the familiar and embrace the untapped wealth that grows from our soil.

Why does history matter now? Understanding our past is crucial as we navigate the future. It reminds us that the wealth of a nation is not only found in the depths of the earth but also in the versatility of its natural endowments. The history of oil in Nigeria is not merely a chronicle of the past; it is a mirror reflecting the potential of our present and the possibilities of our future.

As we turn the pages of this narrative, we make a transition from the annals of history to the contemporary exploration of natural oils. The stage is set for a new chapter in Nigeria's energy saga, one where the bounty of the land offers a beacon of hope and innovation.

Imagine fields upon fields of palm, soybean, and groundnut plantations, their oils ripe for the pressing. These are not just crops; they are vessels of energy, each one holding the key to powering not just automobiles but also the very heart of a nation eager to redefine its destiny.

What if the key to energy independence lay in the oils that we have long used for cooking and traditional medicine? Could these same oils fuel the engines of our cars, buses, and trucks, reducing our carbon footprint and charting a course toward a greener, more sustainable future?

The answer lies etched in the landscape itself, a map of natural reserves waiting to be charted. In Nigeria, the geographical distribution of oil-bearing crops stretches across the nation, from the humid rainforests of the south to the savannas of the north. Each region boasts its own variety of oil-rich flora, a testament to the country's diverse ecological tapestry.

The southern states, with their tropical climate, are the stronghold of the oil palm belt, where the dense groves of palm trees yield the precious red palm oil. As we delve into the heart of these regions, the scent of the oil is as palpable as the history that permeates the air. The southeastern state of Akwa Ibom, the lush landscapes of Ondo, and the fertile grounds of Cross River stand as sentinels of the palm oil legacy, their history intertwined with the very essence of the crop they cultivate. Rockson Rapu devoted personal time in the mid-eighties to tour the vast oil palm plantations in Cross River and Akwa Ibom States, during his business trips to Pamol Nigeria in those days of Natural Rubber Latex research and development. His secondary education at Federal School of Arts and Science, Ondo, also exposed him to the dense plantations in Ondo State.

Moving northward, the central states present a different scene. Here, the land is adorned with vast expanses of soybean and groundnut fields, their golden blooms reaching for the sun. The state of Benue, often hailed as the nation's food basket, is a patchwork of soybean cultivation, while Kano and Kaduna's fame is rooted in their rich groundnut pyramids.

Each of these oils, unique in its properties and potential, offers a piece of the puzzle in our quest for sustainable energy. The challenge now is to harness these resources, to transform them from mere agricultural commodities into the lifeblood of the nation's automobiles.

But how do we make this leap from fertile fields to fuel tanks? The process is as intricate as it is inspiring. Through the alchemy of science and the dedication of researchers, the oils are extracted, refined, and tested, their energy harnessed in a symphony of sustainability and innovation.

As we navigate this complex terrain, questions arise, begging to be answered. How can we ensure the sustainable cultivation of these crops without compromising the integrity of our environment? What technologies must we develop to efficiently convert these natural oils into viable biofuels?

The path forward is not without its obstacles, but the promise it holds is as boundless as the Nigerian spirit. In the chapters that follow, we will explore the intricacies of oil extraction, the science of biofuel production, and the policies that must guide our journey toward a sustainable energy future.

For now, let us stand amidst the oil reserves of Nigeria, marveling at the potential that lies within each seed and each fruit. It is here, on this map of green gold, that we begin to chart a course toward a future powered by the very essence of our land— a future where oil serves not just to function, as the title of this book suggests, but to flourish.

Oil Types and Traits

In the fertile embrace of Nigeria's diverse landscapes, an unassuming yet transformative revolution brews, one that could redefine the country's trajectory toward sustainable energy. As our narrative unfolds, we find ourselves delving deeper into the verdant abundance of natural oils, each a character in this unfolding story of innovation and resilience. It is within these oils that we may unearth a treasure trove of potential, a natural elixir that could propel our automobiles and power our electricity generators.

Before us lies a list, not of mundane items, but of nature's liquid jewels, poised to ignite a renaissance of renewable energy within Nigeria's borders. These are not just substances; they are symbols of possibility, each with a story to tell and a role to play in the grand scheme of energy transformation.

Plant oils can be classified into edible oils and non-edible oils. Various edible plant oils such as palm oil, palm kernel, canola, sunflower, and coconut oil have been studied as feedstock for biodiesel production. In order to serve as a potential feedstock for biodiesel production, the plant source should contain high oil content with favorable fatty acid composition. These plants should be able to grow easily with low material input such as water, pesticides, and fertilizers so that the cost of feedstock can be reduced. In order to continue cultivating the source, they should have a definite developing season. They should be able to develop on grounds that are not attractive for agriculture or cultivate in the off-season of regular ware crops in order to minimize the land rivalry with the development of food. Traditional feedstock for biodiesel production is produced from edible plant oils, for example, rapeseed oil in Europe, soybean oil in the United States, palm oil in Southeast Asia, and coconut oil in the Philippines.

Red Palm Oil, Soybean Oil, Groundnut Oil, Coconut Oil, Rubber Seed Oil, and Jatropha Oil—these are the protagonists of our tale, each with unique traits and secrets waiting to be unlocked. They are more than mere extracts; they are the embodiment of Nigeria's rich biodiversity and the key to its sustainable future.

Red Palm Oil: The Lush Legacy of the South

Dominating the oil palm belt of Nigeria, the vibrant red of palm oil stands as a testament to the region's agricultural prowess. Extracted from the fruit of the Elaeis guineensis, this oil is steeped in history and potential. But what makes it so special? Its high yield and versatility place it at the forefront of the biofuel conversation.

Researchers have found that the saturated fatty acids in palm oil can be converted into biodiesel through a process known as trans-esterification. This biofuel burns cleaner than conventional diesel, emitting fewer greenhouse gases and helping to mitigate the impacts of climate change. In the bustling streets of Lagos, a few experimental buses now hum with engines fueled by this very oil, their tailpipes exhaling a future less reliant on fossil fuels.

Soybean Oil: The Central States' Golden Bloom

Amidst the food basket of the nation, soybean fields stretch toward the horizon, their oil-rich seeds harboring untapped energy. Soybean oil, characterized by its light color and mild taste, is more than just a kitchen staple. Its low saturated fat content makes it a healthier alternative for consumption and an excellent candidate for biodiesel production.

Testimonials from local farmers in Benue state speak of the crop's dual purpose, providing both nutrition and potential energy. With proper investment in extraction and refining technologies, these golden fields could fuel not just the bodies of the people but also the engines of progress.

Groundnut Oil: The Northern Pyramids of Promise

Once a symbol of wealth and export for the northern states, groundnut oil is poised to reclaim its place in Nigeria's narrative. This oil, pressed from the kernels of harvested groundnuts, carries a distinctive flavor and a high smoking point, making it ideal for cooking. But beyond the culinary lies its capacity as a biofuel source.

Studies in Kano and Kaduna showcase pilot projects where groundnut oil has been successfully converted into biodiesel, providing a glimmer of hope for a region eager to diversify its agricultural economy. These pyramids of promise, if leveraged correctly, could form the cornerstone of a sustainable energy infrastructure.

Coconut Oil: The Coastal Treasure

In the coastal enclaves where the ocean kisses the land, the coconut palm thrives, its fruit yielding an oil both versatile and valuable. Coconut oil, with its unique composition of medium-chain fatty acids, has garnered attention for its potential in both health and energy sectors.

Evidence of its dual benefits comes from the sandy shores of Lagos, where local communities use the oil for medicinal purposes and, increasingly, as a fuel alternative. With further research and development, these coastal groves could become the wellspring of a biofuel revolution, their bounty powering engines and empowering communities.

Jatropha Oil: The Hardy Harbinger

Jatropha curcas, a plant that grows with little water or care, offers an oil that may be the dark horse of Nigeria's biofuel race. Its seeds, once considered a mere byproduct of the plant's growth, are now recognized for their oil content, which can be converted into high-quality biodiesel.

The resilience of Jatropha makes it an attractive option for cultivation in arid regions, presenting a beacon of hope for sustainable energy even in the most challenging environments. Anecdotes from small-scale farmers in the northern savannas speak volumes of the plant's potential, painting a picture of a future where barren lands bloom with the seeds of energy independence.

Rubber Seed Oil

Rockson Rapu still remembers those big dreams while representing his organization at the Research Institute in Iyanomo, Nigeria. Dreams like extracting oil from the rubber seed, which is quite a common substrate. Refining this oil finds use as a replacement for imported linseed oil in Nigerian paints, leather refining and glazing, putty, and cosmetics.

In the Far East, rubber seed oil has found use in the paint industry as a semidrying oil, in the manufacture of soap, to produce linoleum and alkyd resins. In medicine it was used as anti-malaria oil, and in engineering as core binder for factice preparation.

The rubber tree is a perennial crop, which belongs to the Euphorbiaceae plant family with the botanical name Hevea brasiliensis. It is a major source of rubber latex. The dehiscent fruit contains about four seeds. The plant yields about 100 to 150 kg seed/ha. This is capable of yielding about 12 000 tons of full-fat rubber seed meal annually (Nwokolo, 1996), which can yield about 5500 tons of rubber seed oil. A study (Morshed et al., 2011) showed that the oil from rubber seed are potential source for biodiesel production in Bangladesh. The biodiesel was produced via a three-step reaction, which covers saponification of oil, acidification of the soap and esterification of the free fatty acids. Recent study (Le et al., 2018) reported the production of biodiesel from rubber seed oil by trans-esterification using a co-solvent of fatty acid methyl esters.

Deeper Exploration

As our exploration of these oils deepens, so too does our appreciation for their intrinsic worth. The transition from theoretical potential to practical application is fraught with challenges, yet it is a journey we must undertake with tenacity and vision. For in these oils, we find not just the means to power our vehicles, but the momentum to drive our nation forward, toward a horizon of green energy and sustainable development.

In the chapters to come, we will navigate the intricate pathways of policy and practice that can transform these natural oils from humble beginnings in the soil to powerful agents of change in the fuel tank. Let us tread this path with eyes wide open, recognizing that within these oils lies the heart of a nation's quest for a greener tomorrow—a quest that begins with the treasures of the earth and the will to use them wisely.

Current Utilizations

In the bustling markets of Abuja, the sizzle of street food frying in groundnut oil carries with it the seeds of a deeper narrative. It is here, among the aromatic stalls and vibrant chatter of daily commerce, where locally sourced natural oils are not merely ingredients for culinary delights but are also being harnessed to drive the engines of industry and innovation.

As Rockson Rapu navigates the vibrant avenues where these oils intersect with everyday life, let's uncover stories of resilience and ingenuity. From the rural farmer to the urban entrepreneur, the main players in this unfolding case study are those who recognize the latent power within these oils and strive to unlock it.

Yet, this journey is not devoid of challenges. The core issue at hand is the transition from traditional uses to advanced applications, particularly in powering automobiles. While the potential is immense, the path is riddled with obstacles such as technological limitations, financial constraints, and a dearth of supportive policies.

The approach to overcoming these challenges is as multifaceted as the oils themselves. Strategies range from grassroots initiatives and local innovations to nation-wide projects aimed at integrating these oils into the energy matrix. For instance, in the heartland of Ondo State, a cooperative has emerged, focusing on converting coconut oil into a biofuel additive. They employ simple, yet effective methods to extract and refine the oil, blending it with diesel in varying proportions to create a more sustainable fuel.

The results are compelling. Initial tests reveal a reduction in emissions and a promise of longer engine life. While the data is still being gathered, the implications are clear: these natural oils can indeed power our vehicles and do so in a way that benefits both the environment and the economy.

Reflecting on these findings, it becomes apparent that while the journey is fraught with difficulties, the rewards are potentially transformative. Criticisms, mainly focused on scalability and efficiency, are not without merit. However, they serve as a catalyst for further innovation rather than as deterrents to progress.

Visual aids, such as charts depicting emission reductions and graphs showing economic benefits, supplement the narrative, offering tangible proof of the positive impact these oils can have.

By connecting these local endeavors to the larger narrative of energy sustainability, it becomes clear that Nigeria is on the cusp of a green revolution. One where its wealth of natural oils can be leveraged to foster a self-sufficient and environmentally conscious society.

As we ponder this transition, a question lingers: How can we amplify these results and replicate success on a national scale?

The journey from oil to function is not a sprint but a marathon—a collective effort that requires patience, persistence, and the willingness to embrace change. Through detailed examinations and reflective insights, this book aims not only to inform but also to inspire action.

Today, in the local markets, groundnut oil may be just a frying medium. But tomorrow, it could be fueling the vehicle that takes a child to school, a family to work, or a nation toward a brighter, cleaner future. The current utilizations of these oils in local industries and daily life are merely the first steps towards a more sustainable and prosperous Nigeria.

As we close this chapter, let us carry with us the understanding that the power to transform our nation lies not just in the vast oil fields of the Niger Delta but also in the modest oil presses of local markets. The potential for greatness can be found in the smallest of seeds, and it is our collective responsibility to nurture these seeds into the towering trees of progress they are destined to become.

Socio-Economic Impact

Beneath the vast skies of Nigeria, a story of transformation is unfolding, one drop of natural oil at a time. These oils, once confined to the kitchen, are now embarking on a journey that could redefine not just the automobile industry, but the very fabric of Nigerian society. In this tapestry of change, each thread represents the potential to weave a new narrative for the nation's socio-economic framework.

In the heart of this discourse lies a central proposition: the use of locally available natural oils for powering automobiles can significantly bolster the Nigerian economy, while simultaneously reshaping social structures. The gravity of this proposition is immense, for it carries with it the dreams and aspirations of a nation on the brink of an energy renaissance.

The first brushstroke of evidence lies in the numbers. Nigeria, a country with an abundant supply of natural oils such as coconut, palm, and groundnut, has the potential to reduce its dependency on imported petroleum products. By harnessing these resources, the country could save precious foreign exchange and create a buffer against the volatility of global oil prices. A study by the Nigerian Institute for Oil Palm Research (NIFOR) suggests that the production and refinement of palm oil for biofuel purposes could generate up to $20 billion annually for the economy.

Delving deeper, the ripple effects of such an industry are far-reaching. Imagine rural communities where oil palm plantations become the nucleus of development. Jobs are created, not just in farming, but in processing, logistics, and retail. The story of Amina, a palm oil farmer in Akwa Ibom state, is illustrative. With the advent of biofuel demand, her income has tripled, allowing her to send her children to school and invest in better farming equipment. This is a microcosm of a larger trend; one where the empowerment of local economies leads to improved education, healthcare, and overall quality of life.

However, every narrative has its counterpoints. Skeptics argue that the diversion of food crops for fuel production could lead to increased food prices and exacerbate food insecurity. They point to the food versus fuel debate, suggesting that prioritizing oil crops for biofuel could harm those who rely on these crops as a staple.

In response, the rebuttal comes armed with innovation. Research indicates that the use of non-edible parts of crops, such as the jatropha plant, could circumvent this issue. Additionally, the development of second-generation biofuels, which use waste biomass, provides a counter-narrative that aligns with both energy and food security goals.

The discourse would be incomplete without acknowledging the environmental advantages. The burning of these natural oils in engines emits fewer greenhouse gases compared to conventional diesel, a fact supported by the Nigerian Environmental Study/Action Team (NEST). This environmental boon could position Nigeria as a leader in the fight against climate change, garnering international goodwill and potentially attracting investment in green technologies.

As we sketch out the broader canvas, let us not forget the cultural impact. The shift towards natural oils is not merely an economic or environmental issue; it also touches the very soul of Nigerian society. It fosters a sense of pride in local ingenuity, a celebration of indigenous knowledge and resources. This is not just about fuel; it's about fueling a national identity grounded in sustainability and self-sufficiency.

To culminate, the evidence, both economic and social, points towards a reinforced assertion: integrating natural oils into Nigeria's energy landscape is a venture ripe with promise. It harbors the potential to create a more robust economy, a healthier environment, and a more cohesive society.

Are we then on the cusp of a new dawn for Nigeria, where the wealth beneath our feet and in our fields is not exploited, but rather, harnessed for the collective good? Could this be the moment where we turn our challenges into opportunities and our resources into reservoirs of hope and prosperity?

With every revolution of an engine powered by natural oils, Nigeria inches closer to answering these questions affirmatively. The journey is long, and the road is fraught with challenges. Yet, the destination—a Nigeria where natural oils do not just function, but thrive and flourish—beckons with the promise of a future built on the ingenuity and resilience of its people.

Environmental Considerations

Nestled in the embrace of Africa, Nigeria's lush landscapes whisper the tales of both abundance and paradox. Here, the earth yields a bounty of natural oils, gifts that hold the promise of sustainable progress. Yet, as engines begin to purr with these green fuels, a specter looms over the nation's verdant expanse. The specter is the ecological cost of oil extraction and use—a shadow that stretches across the Nigerian soil, threatening to taint the waters and mar the air.

The extraction of natural oils, while a beacon of economic hope, casts a long shadow over Nigeria's environment. The problem is multifaceted, with the potential to disrupt ecosystems, pollute water sources, and degrade fertile land. The very act of cultivating vast tracts of land for oil crops can lead to deforestation, soil erosion, and loss of biodiversity. If left unchecked, these practices could rob Nigeria not only of its natural beauty but of its ecological stability as well.

The consequences of such environmental neglect are dire. Soil stripped of its nutrients saps the vitality from future harvests, threatening food security. Polluted rivers become silent graveyards for aquatic life, severing the lifelines of communities that depend on them. The air, heavy with the fumes of irresponsible practices, could choke the very breath of progress.

But what if there were another way? A solution that harmonizes the drumbeats of industry with the gentle rhythms of nature? The answer lies in sustainable extraction practices—methods that respect the earth and safeguard its treasures for generations unborn.

The implementation of this green strategy begins with education. Farmers and corporations alike must be schooled in the ways of conservation agriculture, learning to work with the land, not against it. Crop rotation, organic fertilizers, and reduced tillage are but a few strokes on the canvas of sustainability. Beyond the fields, the refining process must also be refined—to contain its emissions, to treat its effluents, to respect the air and water that cradle life.

Evidence of the effectiveness of such practices already dances on the breeze. Projects that embrace permaculture and agroforestry have shown that yields can be sustained without the heavy hand of environmental degradation. In other climes, success stories abound of lands once barren now bursting with life, of waters once poisoned now pure, of skies once smoggy now clear.

Yet, the path of progress is not a one-way street. Other solutions beckon with the allure of possibility. Could the integration of solar and wind power reduce the reliance on fossil fuels in the extraction process? Will Maxwell Chikumbutso's green energy technology which converts radio frequencies directly into clean and renewable energy, help to cut down on the pollution of the environment? Might the development of biodegradable lubricants and the recycling of waste oil minimize environmental impact? These alternatives, each a thread in the tapestry of sustainability, merit exploration.

As the engines of change hum with the viscous gold of natural oils, let us not be deaf to the questions that need asking. Are we nurturing the land that feeds us? Are we protecting the waters that sustain us? Are we preserving the air that surrounds us?

The rhythm of solutions beats steadily—sustainable farming, cleaner production, alternative energies. Each beat is a step towards a Nigeria that flourishes, not flounders, in the face of ecological challenges.

The road ahead is paved with choices. With every turn of the soil, with every drop of oil, Nigeria holds the power to script its environmental legacy. Will it be a tale of reverence for the earth, or a cautionary account of lost splendor?

The engines of progress wait with bated breath, ready to roar to life with the oils that are Nigeria's pride. Yet, they whisper a silent plea: Let them run not on the ruin of nature, but on the respect for it.

So, as the sun sets on the Nigerian horizon, casting long shadows of the day's labour, let us look to the coming dawn. A dawn where natural oils do more than power automobiles—but power a movement. A movement towards a Nigeria that blossoms in harmony with the earth, an emblem of sustainability, a testament to the balance between industry and environment.

And there, beneath the vast skies of Nigeria, the narrative continues to unfold, one drop of natural oil at a time, each drop a promise—a promise of progress, a promise of preservation, a promise of a future where Nigeria thrives, cradled by an environment as resilient and enduring as the spirit of its people.

Chapter Three

Oils with Potential: A Comparative Analysis

Oil Comparison Metrics

In the pursuit of innovation within the automotive industry, the intriguing concept of using natural oils as fuel beckons a comprehensive understanding of the various oils available. As we delve into the realm of biofuels, we are met with an array of terms that might seem esoteric to the uninitiated. Yet, these terms are the bedrock of knowledge necessary to discern the suitability and efficiency of oils as alternative energy sources.

We embark on this analytical journey by enumerating the key terms that will guide our exploration: viscosity, energy content, cetane number, flash point, cold filter plugging point (CFPP), and biodegradability. Each carries weight in determining the performance and environmental impact of oil as fuel.

Viscosity, the measure of a fluid's resistance to flow, is paramount when considering oil for engines. Picture honey and water; honey flows sluggishly due to its higher viscosity, while water glides effortlessly. An oil's viscosity affects how it moves through an engine, impacting fuel efficiency and wear on engine parts. Oils with low viscosity at cold temperatures aid in easy starting and reduce strain on the battery and starter motor. Conversely, an oil that retains its viscosity at high temperatures provides a protective film over engine components, minimizing wear.

Energy content, the amount of energy packed within a given volume or mass of fuel, is the powerhouse of our discussion. It is the explosive burst of a sprinter off the blocks, propelling vehicles forward. High energy content oils provide more mileage, making them an attractive option for fuel economy.

Next, we encounter the cetane number, which measures the combustion quality of diesel fuel during compression ignition. It is the spark that ignites the fuel, the catalyst for the engine's roar to life. Oils with higher cetane numbers offer smoother engine performance, reduced emissions, and quicker start-ups in cold weather.

Flash point denotes the temperature at which an oil produces enough vapor to ignite in air. Imagine a candle; the wax must heat to a certain point before the wick catches flame. Similarly, a higher flash point ensures safety by reducing the risk of accidental ignition outside the engine.

The cold filter plugging point, an indicator of how well an oil flows at low temperatures, is akin to an athlete's performance in harsh winter conditions. Oils that solidify or gel at cold temperatures can clog filters and lines, leading to engine starvation and possible failure. The lower the CFPP, the better the oil performs in the cold.

Lastly, biodegradability represents an oil's ability to break down naturally and return to the earth. This term cradles the essence of our environmental responsibility. Oils that are readily biodegradable minimize their footprint, contributing to a cleaner environment.

Can you picture an oil that flows through an engine like a river coursing through a valley, brimming with energy, igniting with precision, and leaving no trace as it integrates back into the environment? This imagery is not merely poetic; it encapsulates the ideals of an exemplary biofuel.

Moving beyond the static definitions, let us weave these terms into the tapestry of everyday life. Viscosity is not just a property of oil; it is the thickness of the syrup we pour on pancakes, the ease with which a pen glides across paper and a measure of the thickness of the Rubber Latex that gels into carpet underlay.

Energy content resonates with the vigor we feel after a hearty meal, the readiness to take on the world. The cetane number parallels the responsiveness of a light switch, a quick flick and the room is aglow. Flash point is the caution with which we handle a hot skillet, aware of the potential for a sizzle and spark. The CFPP mirrors the anticipation of a car's engine turning over on a frosty morning, the relief when it hums to life. Biodegradability echoes our desire to leave no trace as we hike through nature, preserving its beauty for generations to come.

As we navigate the intricate landscape of alternative fuels, it becomes clear that the metrics for evaluating oils are not just dry numbers and scientific concepts. They are imbued with life, with relevance to the experiences we encounter daily.

One cannot help but marvel at the symphony of interactions between these metrics and their role in the grander scheme. They are the unsung heroes in the transition to sustainable energy, the silent champions of an eco-conscious future. And though this discourse concludes without a definitive ending, it does so with the understanding that the journey of discovery is far from over.

The Leading Contenders

The quest for sustainable energy sources has led us to the verdant fields and lush forests of Nigeria, a land where the potential for natural oil production remains as rich as the soil from which it springs. As the narrative unfolds, we stand on the brink of a revelation, poised to unveil the leading contenders among Nigeria's natural oils—those that hold the greatest promise for powering automobiles and attracting the gaze of the global market.

In the forthcoming passages, we will delve into an inventory of these top oils, each one a testament to Nigeria's agricultural wealth and industrial potential. Their significance cannot be overstated, for they represent not just commodities, but keys to unlocking a greener future and a more sustainable economy.

The List:

1. Palm Oil

2. Soybean Oil

3. Groundnut Oil

4. Coconut Oil

5. Rubber Seed Oil

6. Castor Oil

Palm Oil

The journey begins with palm oil, the veritable king of oils within the Nigerian landscape. This oil, derived from the fruit of the oil palm tree, is a beacon of versatility and energy density.

Detail Expansion:

Palm oil's rich, reddish hue mirrors its robust composition, imbued with a high energy content that translates into a formidable source of biofuel. Its viscosity, akin to a gentle river, strikes a balance that ensures smooth flow within an engine's veins.

Evidence and Testimonials:

Supported by extensive research and trials, palm oil has emerged as a front-runner in renewable energy studies. Farmers and industrialists alike herald its yield per hectare as unrivaled, a claim substantiated by the fact that oil palm trees are capable of producing up to ten times more oil than other leading oil crops.

Practical Applications:

On the roads, vehicles powered by palm oil derivatives demonstrate a marked improvement in emissions, casting a smaller shadow upon the environment. The promise of palm oil extends to its economic ripple effects, with Nigeria poised to become a powerhouse in the export of this golden resource.

Seamless Transition:

While palm oil stands tall, there is another contender that weaves itself into the fabric of Nigeria's energy tapestry with equal tenacity.

Soybean Oil

Next, we turn our gaze to soybean oil, a fluid treasure extracted from the humble soybean, a legume that has found a welcoming home in Nigeria's agricultural sector.

Detail Expansion:

Soybean oil's lower viscosity at cold temperatures makes it a winter's friend, eager to start engines, without the groan of resistance. Its cetane number whispers of smooth ignitions and a gentleness on machinery, a silent guardian against the harshness of wear and tear.

Evidence and Testimonials:

Farmers attest to the soybean's resilience, thriving in a variety of soils and climates, an adaptability which ensures a steady supply of this precious oil. Studies have shown that soybean oil can be transformed into a biodiesel that burns cleaner than conventional diesel, reducing particulate emissions that cloud our skies.

Practical Applications:

In practice, soybean oil-based biofuels have carved a niche in the energy market, offering a sustainable alternative that does not require modifications to existing diesel engines. Its role in reducing greenhouse gas emissions is not merely theoretical but a tangible stride toward a cleaner future.

Seamless Transition:

From the fields of soy, we journey to the plots of groundnuts, where another oil awaits its turn in the limelight.

Groundnut Oil

Groundnut oil, pressed from the seeds of the groundnut plant, enters the arena with a subtlety that belies its strength.

Detail Expansion:

Its composition is a marvel of moderate viscosity and high energy content, a harmonious blend which lends itself well to the demands of an engine. The cetane number of groundnut oil hints at reliable performance, a steady hand in the combustion process.

Evidence and Testimonials:

Agricultural experts champion the groundnut as a crop that not only provides oil but also enriches the soil with nitrogen, a boon for crop rotation practices. When converted to biofuel, groundnut oil has been praised for its high oxidative stability, offering a longer shelf life and resilience against degradation.

Practical Applications:

Vehicles utilizing groundnut oil biodiesel exhibit a reduction in carbon monoxide and hydrocarbon emissions, a breath of fresh air for urban centers grappling with pollution.

Seamless Transition:

As we explore these oils, let us not forget the coastal whisper of coconut palms, swaying with secrets of their own.

Coconut Oil

Coconut oil, with its exotic origins and sweet aroma, joins the ranks of Nigeria's top natural oils with an air of tropical mystique.

Detail Expansion:

Coconut oil's medium-chain fatty acids provide a unique advantage, offering a cetane number that is favorable for combustion. Its viscosity is a dance between fluidity and stability, ensuring protection and performance within the engine.

Evidence and Testimonials:

Farmers in coastal regions speak of the coconut's generosity, yielding not only oil but a plethora of by-products that sustain local communities. Research into coconut oil's use as a biofuel reveals a high flash point, ensuring safety in handling and storage.

Practical Applications:

On the road, coconut oil-based biodiesel stands as a beacon of potential, with studies indicating lower exhaust emissions and a significant reduction in engine noise, promising a quieter and cleaner driving experience.

Seamless Transition:

From the coast, we turn inland, where the Rubber Plantations flourish in the Southern part especially in the Niger Delta.

Rubber Seed Oil

Next, we look at the much neglected Rubber Seed Oil, another liquid treasure extracted from the obscure but beautiful rubber seed.

A rubber seed has an average weight of 3–5 g, of which about 40 percent is kernel, 35 percent shell, and 25 percent moisture. Oil content in the kernel ranges from 35 to 38 percent.

Detail Expansion:

Rubber Seed Oil's lower viscosity at cold temperatures also makes it a winter's favourite, eager to start engines without stress. Its cetane number enables smooth ignitions and a gentleness on machinery.

Evidence and Testimonials:

Rubber farmers confirm that rubber plantations are now easier to maintain with shorter gestation periods. They testify to the tree's resilience, thriving in a variety of soils and climates. Studies much recently have revealed the use of calcined eggshells impregnated with Al_2O_3 as a heterogeneous catalyst for the conversion of rubber seed oil to biodiesel that burns cleaner than conventional diesel, reducing particulate emissions that pollute the environment.

Practical Applications:

Rubber Seed oil-based biofuels can also carve a niche in the energy market if given a chance. Its role in reducing greenhouse gas emissions is a practical step towards a cleaner environment and the resurrection of the Rubber and Latex industry.

Seamless Transition:

From the Rubber Plantations scattered everywhere in Niger Delta, we move on to the drought resistant castor fields, where another oil awaits its turn in the limelight.

Castor Oil

The narrative culminates with castor oil, an underdog whose time in the spotlight is long overdue.

Detail Expansion:

Castor oil's high viscosity is a double-edged sword—it offers excellent lubrication but requires careful blending to ensure optimal flow at lower temperatures. Its high energy content, however, positions it as a heavyweight in the realm of biofuels.

Evidence and Testimonials:

Farmers who have embraced the castor plant extol its drought resistance, a trait that promises a reliable harvest even in the face of climate challenges. Castor oil's potential as a biofuel is backed by scientific studies, which highlight its exceptional lubricity, reducing wear on engine components.

Practical Applications:

Beyond its theoretical prowess, castor oil has demonstrated real-world merit, with tests showing an improved lubrication and a marked decrease in the wear and tear of engines. It stands as a symbol of untapped potential, a natural resource awaiting its turn to drive innovation and industry.

As the chapter closes on the exploration of Nigeria's leading natural oils, a question lingers in the air: How will these oils shape the future of energy and mobility? The answer lies not just in the pages of research but in the willingness to embrace change, to turn the wheel toward a horizon lined with renewable resources. These oils are more than just substances; they are characters in a story of transformation—a tale of a nation's journey from oil to function.

Chapter Four

Case Studies of Success

Tucked away in the fertile expanses of Nigeria, where the sun graces the land with its warmth, a movement took root. Here, amidst a tapestry of green, local oils began their quiet revolution, fueling not only machines but also the dreams of a nation poised for change.

In a small community in the heart of Nigeria, a cooperative of farmers and engineers united under a singular vision: to transcend traditional energy paradigms and harness the power of local oils for transportation. This community, once reliant on imported fuels, brimmed with untapped resources, each waiting to be woven into the fabric of innovation.

At the forefront stood a collective of determined individuals. Among them was Aisha, a botanist whose intimate knowledge of oil crops had been passed down through generations, and Chinedu, a mechanical engineer with a knack for retrofitting engines to run on alternative fuels. Their collaboration was the catalyst for what would soon be a case study in success.

The challenge was daunting. The community needed to break free from the shackles of dependency on traditional fuel sources, which were not only costly but also environmentally taxing. The goal was to create a self-sustaining model that could be replicated across Nigeria, turning local oils into a linchpin of transportation and commerce.

The approach was multifaceted. Aisha's expertise guided the selection of oil crops best suited for the region, focusing on those that could thrive with minimal environmental impact. Chinedu, meanwhile, spearheaded the development of engine modifications that could accommodate the unique properties of these oils. The cooperative also invested in training local farmers to cultivate these crops, providing them with the tools and knowledge to enhance yield and quality.

The results were nothing short of revolutionary. The first vehicle, powered by a blend of palm and soybean oils, roared to life, its engine humming a tune of possibility. With each passing day, more automobiles joined the chorus, each one a testament to the community's ingenuity and perseverance.

Data soon revealed a dramatic reduction in carbon emissions, and the economic benefits rippled through the community. Farmers, once struggling to find a market for their crops, now had a steady demand. Mechanics carved out new livelihoods in converting and maintaining biofuel-powered engines.

Reflecting on this journey, it is clear that the path was not without its obstacles. Skeptics had doubted the viability of local oils as a fuel source, and there were technical hurdles to overcome in refining and blending the oils for optimal engine performance. Yet, through a combination of traditional wisdom and modern technology, these hurdles were surmounted.

Visual aids, such as charts depicting the drop in emissions and graphs illustrating the economic growth, served to underscore the tangible impact of this venture. They were more than mere visuals; they were emblems of progress.

This case study is a microcosm of a larger narrative, one that underscores the viability of local oils as a sustainable energy source. It speaks to the heart of the book's premise: the transformative power of looking inward, to the riches beneath our feet and the ingenuity within our communities, to power the future.

As we behold this tale of triumph, a question lingers: What other untapped potential lies within reach? What other stories of success await their turn to be told? This is not merely a rhetorical query but a call to action. It is an invitation to dream, to innovate, and to redefine the boundaries of what is possible.

The road ahead is long, and the journey is complex. Yet, if a small community in Nigeria could redefine its destiny with the humble oil crop, what might be achieved on a global scale? The answer lies in the resolve to venture forth into the unknown, armed with the knowledge that from oil, we can indeed function.

Palm Oil versus Other Oils

In the heart of Southeast Asia, vast swathes of plantation stretch towards the horizon, a sea of verdant fronds swaying to an ancient rhythm. Here lies the dominion of palm oil, a resource as controversial as it is versatile. But is it the panacea for our energy woes, or does its promise wane when juxtaposed with other natural oils in the quest to power automobiles? Let us delve into a comparison that may shine a light on this enigmatic contender.

What is the merit of comparing palm oil to its counterparts such as soybean, rapeseed, and sunflower oils? The intent is clear: to unravel the complexities of each oil's capacity to sustainably power the engines of progress. By establishing a set of criteria—energy efficiency, environmental impact, economic viability, and scalability—we lay the foundation for a fair and insightful analysis.

Through the lens of energy efficiency, palm oil stands tall. Its high yield per hectare dwarfs that of soybean and sunflower, making it a juggernaut in terms of potential output. Imagine a single hectare of palm oil plantation producing up to ten times the amount of oil as its soybean counterpart. Here, palm oil's prowess is undeniable, its bountiful harvest a testament to the efficiency of nature's design.

Yet, as we delve deeper, the waters become murkier. The environmental narrative of palm oil is marred by deforestation and habitat loss, casting a long shadow over its benefits. Contrast this with the more sustainable cultivation practices of rapeseed and sunflower oils in certain regions, and the dichotomy becomes stark. Can the promise of palm oil's efficiency be reconciled with the specter of ecological degradation? The question hangs heavy, a pendulum swaying between progress and preservation.

But what of the economic argument? Here, palm oil's affordability and established supply chains present a compelling case. It is a boon for developing nations, where the cost-effective production of palm oil can stir the wheels of industry and uplift communities. Contrast this with the more expensive cultivation and processing of other oils, and palm oil's allure strengthens.

Yet, one cannot ignore the scalability of these oils. While palm oil reigns in the tropics, soybean and rapeseed are the stalwarts of temperate climes. The versatility of these crops, able to be grown in diverse geographies, offers a flexibility that palm oil cannot match. A map dotted with the varied landscapes of these crops' cultivation is a mosaic of potential, each region contributing its unique strengths to the global tapestry.

Do visual aids help to crystallize these comparisons? Certainly, bar graphs juxtaposing yields, pie charts illustrating land use, and line graphs tracking carbon footprints bring an immediacy to the data, a visual anchor to our discourse.

And what of the insights gleaned from this comparative exercise? They reveal a complex interplay of factors that challenge any simplistic verdict. Palm oil's efficiency is marred by its environmental toll, while the more sustainable profiles of other oils grapple with issues of economic and energy output. It is a reminder that in the quest for sustainable energy solutions, trade-offs are inevitable, and perfection remains elusive.

In our contemporary world, where the drumbeat of climate change grows ever louder, the relevance of this discussion cannot be overstated. As nations grapple with the need to reduce carbon emissions, the choice of energy sources becomes not just an economic or environmental issue, but an existential one.

Imagine, if you will, a world where automobiles glide silently along, their engines powered by the most sustainable of oils. Can we envision a future where palm oil's potential is harnessed without the stain of ecological harm, or will the mantle pass to other oils, their cultivation refined to meet the insatiable demand for energy?

We stand at a crossroad, the paths before us diverging in the wood. The decision of which route to take is not to be made lightly, for it carries with it the weight of future generations. As we ponder this choice, let us not be paralyzed by indecision but rather emboldened by the knowledge that from oil, we can indeed function, provided we tread wisely upon the Earth that yields it.

Market Viability Analysis

In a world teeming with innovation and an unyielding quest for sustainable energy, the market demand for natural oils as alternative fuels is a subject that warrants rigorous scrutiny. As we peer into the vast potential of locally sourced natural oils to power our automobiles, we must grapple with the question: what is their economic viability on a global stage?

This market viability analysis seeks to unearth the financial underpinnings of integrating natural oils into the automotive industry's fuel repertoire. The assertion here is clear: if these oils are to succeed, they must do so not only on the merits of sustainability and efficiency but also by proving economically sound in the global market.

The primary evidence supporting our claim is rooted in the current global energy trends. Reports indicate a burgeoning interest in biofuels, with the market for biodiesel alone expected to reach over $44 billion by 2026. This surge is fueled by the increasing stringency of environmental regulations and a collective push toward carbon neutrality. Locally sourced natural oils, with their lower carbon footprint, stand poised to capture a share of this lucrative market.

As we delve deeper, we find that certain regions have already embraced these oils with open arms. In Brazil, for example, soybean oil has become a cornerstone of their biofuel industry, bolstering the nation's energy security while also providing farmers with a viable economic outlet for their crops. The detailed examination of Brazil's model reveals a compelling case for the economic viability of natural oils, where government support and infrastructure investment have paved the way for a thriving market.

However, the path forward is not without its obstacles. Counter-evidence arises from concerns about the scalability of natural oil production and the potential for food prices to soar as cropland is diverted from food to fuel production. Critics argue that the mass adoption of natural oils could strain food supply chains and elevate costs, creating a dilemma between fueling cars and feeding populations.

In response to these concerns, a rebuttal emerges from the advancements in agricultural technology and crop yields. By utilizing non-arable land for energy crop cultivation and improving crop oil content through genetic engineering, it is possible to mitigate the impact on food supplies. Additionally, exploring multi-use crops that provide both food and fuel can create a synergistic effect, boosting economic viability.

Further supporting evidence comes from the technological advancements in engine design, which allow for greater compatibility with various natural oils. Modern engines can now run on a spectrum of biofuels with minimal modifications, reducing the barrier to entry for these alternatives in the automotive sector.

As we draw this analysis to a close, the reinforced assertion stands firm: the global market viability of locally sourced natural oils is not only conceivable but also compelling. With a steady increase in demand for eco-friendly fuels, supportive government policies, and technological innovations, these oils have the potential to carve out a significant niche in the automotive fuel market.

Imagine, if you will, a future where the scent of fried food on city streets is not from the local diner, but from the exhaust of passing cars, their engines humming softly on the energy provided by repurposed cooking oil. Envision fleets of transport trucks traveling cross-country, their diesel engines replaced by ones powered by clean-burning, plant-derived oils. Can we, as a global society, rise to the occasion and make this vision a reality?

The rhythm of progress beats steadily, and the voice of innovation is unrelenting. As the world looks on, the question remains: will the market embrace these natural oils with the fervor of a populace yearning for sustainability, or will they remain but a footnote in the annals of energy history? The answer lies in our collective hands, as we steer the wheel of industry towards a horizon decorated with the promise of a cleaner, more sustainable future.

Chapter Five

Palm Oil: The Golden Crop

Historical Significance of Palm Oil

In the grand tapestry of human endeavor, few resources have woven as intricate a historical filament as palm oil. This golden elixir, flowing from the fruit of the oil palm, has been a mainstay in the livelihoods of millions, shaping economies, cultures, and environments across the globe.

Let us embark upon a journey through time, tracing the roots of palm oil back to the lush landscapes of West Africa. The oil palm, Elaeis guineensis, is native to this verdant region, where it has thrived amid the rainforests and along the riverbanks for millennia. Its earliest use was likely for subsistence, its rich oil providing vital nutrition for the indigenous communities.

As the dawn of civilization cast its light upon the world, so has the understanding and utilization of palm oil evolved. Archaeological excavations near Abydos, one of ancient Egypt's oldest cities, revealed palm oil in tombs dating back to 3000 BCE, suggesting its esteemed role even in the ceremonious practices of antiquity.

The story of palm oil is, in many ways, the story of human ingenuity and expansion. With the age of exploration, European traders set sail, their compasses spinning toward new horizons. When they reached the coasts of West Africa in the 15th century, they encountered a commodity that would soon become a linchpin in international trade—palm oil.

The timeline of palm oil's rise to prominence is punctuated by key milestones. The industrial revolution was one such watershed moment. The demand for a lubricant for machinery and a substitute for tallow in candle making led to a surge in palm oil imports to Britain. By the mid-19th century, palm oil had become a significant import, with West Africa providing the lion's share.

Do images not speak a thousand words? Envision, through historical prints and sketches, the bustling ports of Lagos and Calabar, awash with barrels of palm oil, ready to cross the oceans. The visual aids here would not only enhance understanding but also breathe life into the historical narrative.

Palm oil's journey is painted with distinct cultural strokes. In Nigeria, the Yoruba, Igbo, and Ibibio people each had their unique methods of extraction and uses for the oil, from cooking to traditional medicine and soap making. Across the continent, variations arose, yet the thread of palm oil's significance remained constant.

With the ticking of the clock into modern times, the narrative of palm oil took on new plots. The 20th century saw a shift. No longer were the smallholder farms the sole contributors to the palm oil story; large-scale plantations began to dot the landscapes of Southeast Asia, particularly Malaysia and Indonesia, reshaping the global market.

Have we not witnessed a revolution of sorts in recent years? Biotechnology and genetic engineering have ushered in high-yield hybrid varieties, increasing production to meet the insatiable global demand. The palm oil of today is found not only in food but also in an array of products, from cosmetics to biofuels.

Yet, not all chapters of this history bask in the golden glow of palm oil. The industry has been marred by controversies, from environmental concerns over deforestation and loss of biodiversity to socio-economic issues such as land rights disputes and labour abuses. These challenges have been turning points, sparking a global conversation on sustainability and ethical production.

In conclusion, one must ponder: what does the future hold for palm oil? As this narrative continues, will we see a harmonious balance struck between the needs of humanity and the preservation of our planet? Only time will reveal the next chapter in the historical significance of palm oil.

Cultivation and Production Insights

Embarking on the journey of palm oil cultivation and production is akin to stepping into a complex orchestra of nature and human effort, where each movement leads to the creation of this versatile commodity. The goal here is clear – to cultivate and produce palm oil sustainably while meeting the growing global demands.

One must start with the prerequisites: fertile land, a tropical climate, oil palm seedlings, agricultural tools, and an understanding of sustainable farming practices. These are the foundation on which a successful palm oil operation is built.

Imagine the expansive plantation, a sea of verdant fronds waving in the humid breeze. The broad overview of the process includes site selection, land preparation, planting, maintenance, harvesting, and finally, milling and refining.

Drifting closer to the earth, let's delve into the details. Site selection must consider soil quality, topography, and access to water. Next, the land is cleared and terraced if necessary, always with a mindful approach to preserving the environment. Planting follows, with rows of oil palm seedlings carefully spaced to allow for mature growth.

Maintenance is a symphony of tasks: fertilizing to nourish the soil, pruning to encourage healthy fronds, and vigilant protection against pests and diseases. The harvest season arrives with a flourish, as ripe bunches of oil palm fruit are collected, a testament to the grower's dedication.

Now, pause and picture the golden oil as it begins to emerge from the fruit. Practical advice for the producer includes regular soil testing to ensure optimal health and the use of organic fertilizers to promote sustainability. Warnings abound, too – beware the overuse of pesticides and the temptation of over-planting, which can lead to soil exhaustion.

Validation of efforts comes through the yield. High-quality oil with a rich color and purity signifies success, as does a thriving ecosystem surrounding the plantation. Should challenges arise, such as lower-than-expected yields or pest infestations, troubleshooting includes consulting with agronomists and considering integrated pest management strategies.

Let's pivot now and reflect. Have you considered the environmental footprint of your consumption? As we journey through the meticulous process of palm oil production, it's essential to recognize the impact each step has on the broader canvas of our planet.

Dotted throughout the narrative are moments that call for emphasis, like the need for sustainable practices to ensure the longevity of both the industry and the environment. These points stand alone, resolute in their importance.

Employing simple language, let us not forget the people behind the scenes – the farmers and workers whose hands shape the destiny of palm oil. Their stories, often untold, are as rich as the oil itself.

Planted within the text, quotations from industry experts and local farmers add depth and authenticity, revealing the human element in the vast mechanism of palm oil production.

"Each palm fruit is a capsule of life, sustaining not just the tree, but the many hands that bring it to the world," muses a seasoned farmer, his life's work etched into the lines of his face.

In the end, let's show the reader the reality of palm oil cultivation and production – the early morning mists hanging over the plantation, the rhythmic sound of fruit being collected, and the heat of the mill as oil is extracted. It's a tapestry of sights, sounds, and smells that tells a story far richer than a mere recounting of facts could ever achieve.

This chapter on cultivation and production not only informs but also invites reflection on the intersection of human enterprise and the natural world. As the narrative of 'Oil to Function' unfurls, may the insights gleaned here illuminate the path forward, both for the industry and for the conscientious reader.

Palm Oil's Unique Properties

In the quest to harness the full potential of natural oils for automobile power, one cannot overlook the extraordinary qualities of palm oil. This oil, drawn from the fruit of oil palm trees, stands as a beacon of versatility in the realm of biofuels. Its unique chemical and physical properties beckon a closer examination, revealing why it holds such promise for the future of sustainable energy.

The essence of grasping palm oil's potential lies in understanding the key elements that define its character. Triglycerides, fatty acid composition, and saturation levels are not merely terms; they are the building blocks of palm oil's functionality. Let us embark on an exploratory journey, unveiling these terms and grasping their significance.

Triglycerides, for instance, form the backbone of palm oil. These molecules, composed of glycerol and three fatty acids, store energy and provide the structural basis for many natural oils. In palm oil, the unique arrangement of these fatty acids contributes to its solid consistency at room temperature, a trait not found in many other vegetable oils.

Delving deeper, one encounters the fatty acid composition, a tapestry woven from a diverse array of acids such as palmitic, stearic, oleic, and linoleic acids. Each fatty acid imparts a distinct characteristic to the oil, influencing melting points, stability, and suitability for various applications. The preponderance of palmitic acid, for instance, lends palm oil its semi-solid state, which is highly advantageous for biofuel production.

Saturation levels further demarcate palm oil from its counterparts. Saturated fats, often maligned in dietary contexts, shine in the realm of biofuels. Their resistance to oxidation grants palm oil a longer shelf life and better performance in engines, where unsaturated oils might falter.

How do these properties translate to the real world? Consider the melting point. Palm oil's semi-solidity at ambient temperatures means that in cooler climates, it might require blending or heating to maintain fluidity in fuel systems. Yet, this same characteristic ensures that palm oil-based biodiesel is less prone to thinning in the heat, a common challenge with other biofuels.

Moreover, palm oil's resistance to oxidation is beneficial for storage and stability, allowing for extended shelf life and reducing the need for preservatives. When ignited in an engine, this stability translates to cleaner burning and a reduction in harmful emissions—an undeniable benefit for our atmosphere.

As we navigate through these technicalities, questions arise. How might the properties of palm oil change when it is processed or blended? What are the implications of these changes for the automotive industry? These inquiries guide our understanding and open doors to innovation.

Yet, amidst this labyrinth of scientific detail, we must not lose sight of the simple truths. Palm oil's utility extends beyond the engines it powers; it is also a source of employment and economic stability for many communities. This multi-faceted impact underscores the oil's significance in both local and global contexts.

Employing vivid imagery, just visualize the golden-hued palm oil as it courses through an engine, its molecules dancing in combustion to release energy. This dance is choreographed by the very properties we have dissected here.

Incorporating direct questions, one may ask: Can you imagine the journey from the tropical plantation to the inner workings of your car's engine? How might the intricate dance of palm oil molecules transform the future of transport?

The exploration of palm oil's unique properties does not conclude with a definitive ending, but rather opens a gateway to further discovery and contemplation. The oil's journey from tree to tank is a narrative punctuated by its robust characteristics, each playing a pivotal role in its suitability as a biofuel.

As palm oil continues to carve its niche in the renewable energy sector, its unique properties stand testament to nature's ingenuity and human innovation. The chapters that follow will build upon this foundation, delving into the practical applications and implications of palm oil in powering our automobiles and shaping our world.

Economic Impact of Palm Oil

Amidst the verdant groves of oil palms that stretch across the Nigerian landscape, a quiet revolution is brewing. This is a revolution that has the potential to steer the country toward a future of economic prosperity and sustainable energy. In Nigeria, the palm oil industry emerges as a formidable player, contributing significantly to the nation's GDP and offering a beacon of hope for economic diversification.

Nestled within this dynamic sector are key players – smallholder farmers, large-scale plantations, processing companies, and government bodies – each interwoven in the fabric of the industry's success. These entities, with their varying scales of operation and objectives, form the mosaic of the palm oil economy in Nigeria.

For decades, the nation has grappled with the challenge of over-reliance on crude oil exports, a volatile market that often leaves the economy susceptible to global price shocks. However, the resurgence of the palm oil sector presents a paradigm shift, an opportunity to harness locally sourced wealth. This is not without its hurdles; inadequate infrastructure, fluctuating market prices, and land tenure issues pose significant challenges to the sector's growth.

The strategic approach to surmounting these obstacles has been multifaceted. The Nigerian government, recognizing the sector's potential, has initiated supportive policies and incentives. These include tax holidays, import restrictions to protect local producers, and funding for research into high-yield palm varieties. Simultaneously, non-governmental organizations and private entities have stepped in to provide training and support to smallholder farmers, ensuring they are equipped with modern farming techniques and sustainable practices.

The results of these concerted efforts are palpable. Data reflects a steady increase in palm oil production, with domestic output rising to meet the demands of both local consumption and international export. The ripple effects of this growth extend far beyond the industry itself, as increased revenue has led to infrastructural developments, job creation, and a boost in related sectors such as transportation and manufacturing.

A closer analysis reveals a nuanced picture. The sector's expansion has indeed propelled economic growth, yet concerns remain regarding environmental sustainability and the equitable distribution of wealth. The large-scale deforestation associated with plantation expansion poses a threat to Nigeria's rich biodiversity, while the benefits of the industry's growth are not always felt by the smallholder farmers at the grassroots level.

Enriching the narrative through visual aids, one might consider the juxtaposition of lush plantations against the backdrop of thriving local communities, each picture telling a story of growth, challenge, and hope.

Delving deeper, the palm oil narrative in Nigeria is interlaced with the broader concepts of renewable energy, environmental stewardship, and economic diversification. As the world shifts its gaze towards cleaner energy sources, the prominence of palm oil as a biofuel feedstock positions Nigeria at the forefront of this global transition.

Yet, a lingering question persists: How can Nigeria balance the scales of economic gain with environmental responsibility and social equity? This conundrum beckons further engagement from stakeholders and forms a critical juncture in the nation's journey toward sustainable development.

As an entrepreneur, Rockson Rapu's vision extends beyond the immediate horizon. It is not just about understanding the current economic impact of palm oil; it is about envisioning a future where the industry serves as a cornerstone for a robust, diversified, and sustainable Nigerian economy. Where every farmer, every worker, and every entrepreneur connected to palm oil can partake in the fruits of their labour, and where the environment is preserved for generations to come.

In this chapter of our exploration, we witness the transformative power of natural resources when leveraged with foresight and responsibility. The story of palm oil in Nigeria is still being written, its chapters unfolding with every harvest, every policy, and every innovation. As we turn the page, we are reminded that the true measure of progress lies not only in economic metrics but in the well-being of the people and the health of the planet they call home.

Potential and Limitations

Amid the verdant landscapes where palm trees sway, the heart of a dilemma throbs with increasing urgency. This dilemma, deeply rooted in the soil of Nigeria's burgeoning palm oil industry, presents a complex challenge that could redefine the nation's trajectory towards a greener automotive future. As engines hum and gears shift, could the same oil that sizzles in frying pans and enriches beauty products also fuel the cars upon which we so heavily rely? The use of palm oil as a biofuel is an enticing prospect, offering a tantalizing glimpse into a future less dependent on fossil fuels. Yet, to consider it a panacea would be to oversimplify a multifaceted issue. The question looms: How does one harness the potential of palm oil for automotive energy without succumbing to the pitfalls that accompany its use?

The primary challenge at hand is one of balance and foresight. The allure of palm oil is undeniable; a renewable resource that can be cultivated with relative ease, promising a substantial reduction in greenhouse gas emissions when compared to traditional fuels. Its potential to invigorate local economies and reinforce energy security cannot be overstated. However, the shadow that falls upon this golden prospect is cast by the environmental and social concerns that its production can entail.

Should we remain passive, the consequences are grim and far-reaching. Deforestation, habitat loss, and the displacement of indigenous communities are but a few of the dark clouds on the horizon. Biodiversity, the very fabric of life, could fray and tear under the strain of vast monoculture plantations. The displacement of food crops by fuel crops could jeopardize food security, an irony that stings in its contradiction.

Is there a way to navigate this minefield of consequences, to extract the essence of the solution without the bitter aftertaste of its drawbacks? Indeed, there are practical solutions at our doorstep, waiting to be ushered in through the gates of innovation and policy.

A beacon of hope lies in the development and implementation of more stringent and sustainable cultivation practices. The Roundtable on Sustainable Palm Oil (RSPO) has laid down criteria that, if adopted on a wider scale, could significantly mitigate the environmental impact. Smallholder inclusivity, zero deforestation commitments, and stringent supply chain monitoring are the cornerstones of this approach.

The journey towards implementation begins with the education and empowerment of local farmers. By providing them with the knowledge and tools to adopt sustainable practices, we not only protect the environment but also enhance their livelihoods. This is a path that leads to certification, opening doors to a global market increasingly sensitive to the origins of its products.

Evidence of the efficacy of these solutions echoes from corners of the world where they have been embraced. In regions adopting RSPO guidelines, there has been a notable decrease in the rate of deforestation and a positive shift in local economic dynamics. The increased yield from sustainable practices often compensates for the reduced land area under cultivation, a win-win scenario that speaks volumes.

Are there other solutions that merit our attention? Most certainly. Diversifying into other non-food-based biofuel feedstocks, such as jatropha or algae, could alleviate some pressure from palm oil. Technological advancements in automotive engines could also reduce the overall demand for biofuel, further easing the burden on palm oil production.

In the stillness of a moment, let us ponder. What if every stakeholder in the palm oil narrative – farmers, corporations, consumers, and governments – were to align their compasses towards sustainability? Could the very act of driving our automobiles be transformed into a gesture of environmental stewardship?

Our quest for answers must be relentless, our commitment unwavering. For within this challenge lies not only a conundrum but an opportunity. An opportunity to reinvent our energy landscape, to sow the seeds of a future where automobiles glide along roads, powered by the essence of nature itself, with the blessings of the earth and its inhabitants.

Let this be more than a fleeting vision. Let it be our collective mission, a testament to human ingenuity and respect for the natural world. The road ahead is long and winding, but with each step taken in earnest, the dawn of a new era in automobile energy comes ever closer.

Chapter Six

Biofuel Revolution: Palm Oil in Automobiles

Biofuel Basics: Understanding the Science

In a world teetering on the brink of an energy crisis, the search for sustainable fuel sources is not just a matter of environmental concern, but one of existential necessity. Enter the realm of biofuels – a beacon of hope in the quest for a greener future. At the heart of this hope lies the humble palm oil, a natural resource that, while mired in controversy, holds untapped potential in the biofuel industry.

Consider the oil that powers your car now. Traditionally, this has been a product refined from the ancient remains of prehistoric organisms – fossil fuels. But as we pivot towards sustainability, biofuels emerge as an alternative. These are fuels derived from living matter, a renewable and potentially less environmentally damaging source of energy. Amongst them, palm oil stands out as a versatile and widely available option.

To truly grasp the essence of biofuels, one must understand their origin. Biofuels are produced from biomass, which can include plant materials and animal waste. They are primarily categorized into two types – bioethanol and biodiesel. Bioethanol is alcohol made by fermenting the sugar components of plant materials and is mostly used as a gasoline supplement. Biodiesel, on the other hand, is produced through a chemical process called trans-esterification, where oils and fats are converted into fatty acid methyl esters, which can be used in diesel engines.

Imagine a farmer harvesting oil palms and the oil extracted from the fruit being used to power a tractor – this is biofuel at work. Brazil's use of sugarcane-derived ethanol is a prime example of bioethanol application, while biodiesel is gaining ground with soybean, rapeseed, and yes, palm oil.

Where some see a solution, others spot a problem. Biofuels, particularly those involving palm oil, have sparked a debate. On one side, proponents argue for biofuels' lower carbon footprint and reduced reliance on fossil fuels. Critics, however, point to deforestation and the resultant biodiversity loss associated with expanding oil palm plantations.

Numbers tell a compelling tale. For instance, the European Union aims for over 10% of all transport fuels to be biofuels by 2026. Moreover, studies have shown that biofuels can reduce greenhouse gas emissions by up to 86% compared to fossil fuels.

Trans-esterification might seem daunting, but it's simply a process where glycerine is separated from the fat or vegetable oil, leaving behind two products – methyl esters (the biofuel) and glycerine (a byproduct used in soaps and other products).

Biofuels, including those derived from palm oil, represent an intriguing intersection of agriculture and energy production. They offer a renewable energy source that could lead to a reduction in carbon emissions and a decrease in the global dependency on fossil fuels. However, the journey towards biofuel integration is complex, laden with environmental and social implications that must be navigated with care.

The narrative of biofuel is constantly evolving, much like the science that underpins it. As we delve deeper into 'Oil to Function', the focus will sharpen on the mechanics of transforming palm oil into a biofuel powerhouse, examining the intricacies and the potential that this golden oil holds in the tapestry of renewable energy sources.

Conversion Processes

Embarking on the journey of converting palm oil into a viable biofuel for the automotive orchestra, we aim to unlock the alchemy that transmutes this golden elixir into a symphony of sustainable energy. Bear witness to a process that marries tradition with innovation, giving birth to a fuel that propels us forward without leaving a scar on Mother Earth's visage.

Before we wade into the waters of transformation, let's marshal our resources. The essentials include high-quality palm oil, a repository of catalysts, methanol, and the heart of the operation—a biodiesel processor. Ancillary yet vital gears in this machinery are the safety equipment and an array of containers and measuring paraphernalia.

Imagine the landscape of conversion as a tapestry woven with various threads of action, each critical to the integrity of the final product. At a glance, the process unfurls in stages: pretreatment of the oil, the reaction of trans-esterification, separation and purification of the biodiesel, and finally, quality assurance tests.

Now, let us delve beneath the surface and dissect these stages, unraveling their complexities. The initial phase, pretreatment, is akin to preparing the canvas for a masterpiece. Contaminants such as water and free fatty acids must be purged from the palm oil. This ensures a pure base, free of impediments that might hinder the ensuing chemical ballet.

With the stage set, we introduce our actors—methanol and a catalyst, commonly sodium hydroxide or potassium hydroxide. The oil, now pristine, is coaxed into a reaction with these substances, breaking its triglyceride chains and giving rise to methyl esters and glycerine. This trans-esterification is a delicate dance, requiring precise temperatures and stoichiometric harmony.

Pause here, and ponder—what good is a product if not pure? The nascent biodiesel must be decanted, separating it from the glycerine byproduct. Washed and dried, the biodiesel emerges, phoenix-like, ready for its ultimate purpose but not before undergoing rigorous testing. Purity and performance are scrutinized; parameters such as viscosity, cetane number, and flash point are but a few of the metrics against which our biofuel is measured.

As with any endeavor of worth, challenges may arise. Incomplete reactions, excessive soap formation, or contamination could mar the process. Fear not, for vigilance and a well-stocked armory of troubleshooting strategies can conquer these foes. Monitor the reaction's progress, maintain the purity of inputs, and the machinery calibrated, for these are the bulwarks against failure.

In the alchemy of conversion, we turn the palm oil—once the simple bounty of nature—into a fuel that powers our journeys without guzzling the essence of future generations. From the fields where palms sway to the engines that roar with renewed vigor, this is the circle of innovation, a testament to human ingenuity and respect for the environment.

And thus, the narrative of 'Oil to Function' continues to unfold, each page a testament to the delicate balance between progress and preservation. Through the pages of this tome, we enlighten and inspire, providing a beacon for those who dare to dream of a world powered not by the relics of the past but by the seeds of today.

Performance Metrics

In our relentless pursuit of alternative fuels, we juxtapose the familiar faces of petrol and diesel with the burgeoning potential of palm oil biofuel and the silent surge of electric vehicles. These actors in the global energy theater play pivotal roles, yet their performances are as varied as the landscapes they traverse. Why compare them, one might ask? The answer lies in the pursuit of a sustainable future, where energy demands harmonize with environmental stewardship.

Our criteria for comparison are multifaceted, encompassing energy efficiency, emissions, cost-effectiveness, and scalability. By these measures, we shall discern the strengths and weaknesses that define our subjects.

Energy efficiency is often the headliner in such evaluations. Petrol and diesel have long set the bar with high energy densities that translate into powerful, long-range travel. Yet, palm oil biofuel is no mere understudy; its renewable nature whispers promises of a sustainable cycle. Electricity, on the other hand, dances to a different rhythm, its efficiency in converting energy to motion unparalleled.

As we draw parallels, we see that both biofuel and fossil fuels share the combustion stage, releasing energy through similar processes. Electric vehicles, meanwhile, sidestep combustion entirely, opting instead for a direct flow of electrons that propels them forward.

Do these similarities mean that palm oil biofuel is merely a green-tinted shadow of its fossil relatives? Far from it. Though they share a stage, palm oil biofuel brings its own flair to the performance, a reduction in carbon emissions that comes from its renewable roots.

Yet, contrast sharpens the image. Diesel and petrol's emissions have long been a specter haunting the environment, contributing to air pollution and climate change. Palm oil biofuel, when sourced sustainably, can curtail these emissions significantly, although its cultivation raises questions of land use and deforestation. Electric vehicles glide onto the scene with an almost ethereal absence of tailpipe emissions, but their environmental impact is tethered to the source of their electricity.

A visual aid, such as a bar graph or pie chart, could elegantly illustrate the stark differences in emissions, or a table comparing energy efficiencies could offer clarity at a glance.

Digging deeper, our analysis unveils that palm oil biofuel's lower emissions do not come at the cost of performance. Indeed, studies suggest that engines run on this golden elixir exhibit a comparable might to their petrol-fueled counterparts. The torque and horsepower tell a story of a robust alternative, capable of shouldering the weight of transportation demands.

But this narrative is not without its twists. The cost of production and fuel availability come into play, shaping the broader implications of each fuel's use. The infrastructure for petrol and diesel is as vast as the oceans, while biofuel and electric charging points are islands still expanding their shores.

What does this mean for the world that hustles and bustles around us? The implications are as profound as the depths of the ocean. A shift toward palm oil biofuel and electricity could signal a new era of energy consumption, one that breathes life into our fight against climate change.

Could the day come when the hum of electric motors drowns out the roar of combustion engines, or when fields of palms become the wellsprings of our travels? The market already responds to these whispers of change, with consumers and manufacturers alike steering the wheel toward sustainability.

And so, the question hangs in the air, palpable as the scent before a rainstorm: Are we witnessing the twilight of the age of oil, or merely a diversification of the players within it? The answer, it seems, lies not in the stars, but in our hands, in the choices we make and the values we champion.

The performance metrics of these fuels are more than numbers; they are the harbingers of a future we are yet to write. As we turn the page on traditional energy sources and look to the horizons of innovation and sustainability, we must ask ourselves: Are we ready to embrace the change, to champion the underdog, and to electrify our intentions with action? The stage is set, the actors poised, and the next act is ours to command.

Infrastructure and Adaptation

Nestled within the intricate tapestry of modern transportation lies a vital, yet often overlooked, thread: infrastructure. The very sinews and bones of our cities, the expansive network of roads, bridges, and fuel stations, have been tailored to the demands of petrol and diesel. But as the tides of change beckon, a new contender emerges: palm oil biofuel. Its advent poses a direct challenge to the status quo, urging a metamorphosis of the existing infrastructure. This nascent fuel source, with its verdant promise of sustainability, begs the question: Are our cities ready to transform in tandem with our ambitions?

The problem is as clear as the crisp lines on a blueprint; our current infrastructure is ill-suited for the widespread adoption of palm oil biofuel. This misalignment threatens to curtail the potential of this green energy source, rendering it a mere footnote in the annals of automotive history. Without intervention, the promise of a cleaner, renewable fuel may dissolve into the ether, a casualty of incompatibility.

Imagine the consequences if this challenge is left unaddressed; a future choked by the fumes of missed opportunities, where innovation is stifled by the inertia of the old ways. A landscape where palm oil biofuel remains a peripheral player, overshadowed by the giants of fossil fuels, its potential sequestered by the very infrastructure that could empower its ascension.

What, then, is the solution to this conundrum? The answer lies in a harmonious blend of foresight, innovation, and strategic planning. The first step is a systematic retrofitting of existing fuel stations, equipping them with dedicated pumps and storage tanks for palm oil biofuel. This will ensure that as vehicles capable of running on this natural elixir proliferate, the fuel is readily available. But the change must not stop there. New stations, designed with an eye towards the future, must rise, monuments to our environmental commitment and technological adaptability.

Implementing such a solution requires a meticulous approach. Legislation must pave the way, incentivizing the transformation of fuel stations. Public and private investments will be the catalysts, financial seeds sown today that will blossom into the forests of change tomorrow. Education campaigns, too, must sweep through cities and country sides alike, cultivating an awareness of the benefits of palm oil biofuel and preparing the populace for this shift.

Evidence of the efficacy of such strategies can be glimpsed in countries that have successfully integrated biofuels into their energy portfolios. Brazil stands as a testament to this, where flex-fuel vehicles flourish and biofuel pumps are as common as their fossil-fueled counterparts. The result? A significant reduction in carbon emissions and a bolstered energy security, a beacon of success for others to follow.

Yet, one must ponder alternative solutions, for prudence dictates that we explore all avenues. Electrification of transport is one such path, with electric vehicles (EVs) gaining momentum. However, the integration of EVs faces its own set of infrastructure challenges, from charging stations to grid capacity. Thus, while EVs represent a parallel path towards sustainability, they do not diminish the urgency of adapting infrastructure for biofuels.

One could argue that a diversified approach, embracing both biofuels and electric vehicles, might be the wisest course. After all, the journey to a sustainable future is not a sprint but a marathon, with many potential routes leading to the finish line.

As we stand at the crossroads of change, we must ask ourselves: Are we willing to undertake the journey of transformation, to lay the groundwork for a future powered by the fruits of the Earth? The answer should resonate with the clarity of dawn's first light, for it is in our hands to shape the roads on which future generations will travel.

The narrative of palm oil biofuel does not end with its production; it extends into the very fabric of our society, woven into the heart of our infrastructure. With careful planning and a collective will, we can ensure that this chapter of our story is one marked by innovation, environmental stewardship, and a bold step towards a greener tomorrow. The question remains, will we drive forth into this new era with determination, or will we idle, prisoners of hesitation, as the world passes us by? The choice is ours, and the time to act is now.

Case Studies: Palm Oil-Powered Vehicles

In the lush expanses of tropical landscapes, palm trees rise with a promise of energy that has begun to fuel more than just local economies. As an entrepreneur who has witnessed firsthand the transformative power of innovation, Rockson Rapu is compelled to share the tales of palm oil's journey from groves to engines, a testament to human ingenuity and the quest for sustainable alternatives.

The horizon of this narrative is painted with the golden hues of palm oil biofuel, a horizon that has seen the dawn of vehicles powered by this natural resource. It is within this context that we delve into the real-world examples, where the rubber meets the road, and palm oil meets the engine.

In a small village in Thailand, the hum of engines harmonizes with the rustling palm fronds. Here, amidst the backdrop of verdant fields and a community bound by tradition, a fleet of tractors rumbles to life, their engines modified to run on locally sourced palm oil. This is not a scene from a utopian novel, but a glimpse into a revolution under the sun.

The main players in this case study are the local farmers, an innovative engineer named Boonsom, and a cooperative that binds them. Engineer Boonsom, with his grease-stained hands and a mind as sharp as the machete he once used to harvest palm fruit, is the visionary who saw potential where others saw waste. The cooperative, a tapestry of local families, provides the structure and support needed to sustain their collective ambition.

The challenge at the heart of this study was clear: how to reduce the reliance on expensive, imported diesel fuel that burdened the farmers' finances and tethered them to the volatility of global oil markets. The answer lay in the very fields that surrounded them—palm oil, abundant and underutilized.

Engineer Boonsom's approach was both simple and revolutionary. He adapted the tractors' engines with rudimentary, yet effective modifications, enabling them to run on pure palm oil. This was not a mere tinkering but a reimagining of energy consumption at the grassroots level.

The results were as palpable as the soil under the farmers' feet. Fuel costs plummeted, and the newfound independence from imported diesel invigorated the community. Data collected over a year showed a 50% reduction in fuel expenses and a significant decrease in carbon emissions, making a compelling case for the wider adoption of palm oil as a biofuel.

However, an analysis of this initiative reveals layers of complexity. There were concerns about the long-term impact on engines not originally designed for palm oil and the potential effects on local ecosystems due to increased demand. Reflecting on these criticisms leads to a broader conversation about the balance between innovation and sustainability.

Visual aids, such as graphs depicting the economic savings and emission reductions, further underscore the tangible benefits of this case study.

These graphical narratives tell a story beyond words, illustrating the positive ripple effects of the initiative.

Connecting back to the larger narrative of palm oil as an alternative fuel source, this case study is more than an isolated success; it represents a microcosm of what could be achieved on a global scale. It underscores the need for infrastructural versatility, community-driven solutions, and policies that encourage the use of renewable energy sources.

As we contemplate this case study, one cannot help but ponder the question: If such success is possible in a small village, what could be achieved if similar strategies were implemented on a global scale? Could this be the spark that ignites a larger movement towards energy independence and environmental responsibility?

In Rockson Rapu's journey as a business consultant, he has seen the power of ideas that germinate in the fertile soil of community need and grow into movements that transcend borders. The case of palm oil-powered vehicles is one such idea, burgeoning with potential, rooted in practicality, and awaiting the collective will to drive it forward. It stands as a beacon, guiding us toward a future where we harness the earth's gifts responsibly and ingeniously.

This exploration is not the end, but rather a single mile on a much longer voyage. As we look to the horizon, where innovation meets tradition, and sustainability becomes not just a goal but a reality, we must ask ourselves: Are we ready to embrace the change that beckons and to become not just passengers but drivers of our collective destiny?

The journey of palm oil from the tree to the tank is a narrative rich with potential, a chapter in the larger story of renewable energy that we are still writing. It is a journey that speaks to our resilience, our creativity, and our unyielding pursuit of a brighter, cleaner tomorrow. Together, let us continue to turn the pages, to explore, and to question, for it is through such endeavors that progress is made, and history is shaped.

Chapter Seven

The Green Advantage

Environmental Impacts: Carbon Footprint Analysis

In the relentless pursuit of environmental sustainability, the quest for cleaner energy sources has brought into sharp focus the potential of natural oils to power our vehicles. As the world grapples with the adverse impacts of climate change, we find ourselves at the precipice of an energy revolution, one that could significantly alter the way we fuel our engines. The shift from traditional fossil fuels to biofuels made from natural oils is not merely a topic of scientific inquiry but a pressing global imperative.

The central proposition we examine here is that palm oil biofuel presents a greener alternative to fossil fuels, with a potential reduction in carbon emissions. This assertion is not without merit; preliminary studies have suggested that biofuels can indeed lead to a smaller carbon footprint. However, to truly understand the implications of this claim, a rigorous analysis of the evidence is necessary.

A primary piece of evidence supporting the use of palm oil biofuel is its renewable nature. Unlike fossil fuels, which are finite and release carbon that has been sequestered for millions of years, palm oil is part of the current carbon cycle. As palm trees grow, they absorb carbon dioxide from the atmosphere, ostensibly offsetting the emissions produced when the oil is burned as fuel. This harmonious cycle of absorption and emission offers a compelling narrative for palm oil's carbon neutrality.

But let us delve deeper into this evidence. The carbon cycle of palm oil is more complex than it first appears. It involves not just the growth and combustion stages but also the land use changes often associated with palm oil cultivation. Peatland or Bogs conversion and Deforestation for palm plantations release significant amounts of stored carbon, which might negate the benefits of its biofuel's lower emissions. This consideration adds layers of nuance to the initial claim and suggests that the reality may not be as straightforward as it seems.

Now, turn your gaze to the counter-evidence. Critics argue that when considering the full life cycle of palm oil production, the environmental benefits shrink substantially. The conversion of biodiverse forests into monoculture plantations has far-reaching ecological ramifications, including habitat loss and a decrease in carbon sequestration potential. Some experts even posit that these factors could cause palm oil biofuel to have a higher carbon footprint than traditional fossil fuels.

In response to these challenges, further clarification is warranted. Proponents of palm oil biofuel point out that sustainable farming practices and technological advancements in biofuel production can mitigate many of the adverse environmental impacts. By adhering to stringent sustainability criteria and using waste materials instead of virgin palm oil, the industry can significantly reduce its carbon footprint.

Can we bolster this argument with additional supporting evidence? Certainly. Research has shown that second-generation biofuels, which include palm oil derivatives, have the potential to reduce greenhouse gas emissions by up to 85% compared to fossil fuels, provided they are produced sustainably. This is a significant figure that cannot be overlooked in the discussion.

As we bring this analysis to a close, it is important to reiterate the initial assertion: palm oil biofuel has the potential to be a less carbon-intensive alternative to fossil fuels. While it is not without its challenges and complexities, when produced responsibly, palm oil biofuel could play a pivotal role in our transition to a more sustainable energy future. The evidence, though multifaceted and sometimes contradictory, leans in favor of a more optimistic view of palm oil's role in reducing our carbon footprint. This is not a black-and-white issue but one that requires careful consideration of all shades of green.

Sustainability Practices

Venturing into the realm of sustainable palm oil cultivation, one envisions a future where lush green plantations not only yield the golden elixir used to power our vehicles but also exemplify an ethos of environmental stewardship. The journey towards such a future is paved with intention, knowledge, and a series of well-crafted steps designed to minimize our ecological footprint while maximizing the benefits of biofuel consumption. Here, we unfurl a tapestry of actions that, when woven together, depict the best practices for sustainable palm oil cultivation and biofuel production.

Firstly, let's clarify our objective: to develop and implement a system of palm oil cultivation that respects and preserves the environment while providing a viable source of biofuel. This is a goal drenched in the sweat of hard work, yet sparkling with the dew of hope for a greener future.

To achieve this vision, we must gather our tools and resources. The prerequisites are multifaceted, encompassing legal, environmental, and social components. We require an understanding of sustainable farming techniques, access to high-quality palm oil seeds, a workforce educated in sustainability practices, and adherence to strict environmental standards such as those set forth by the Roundtable on Sustainable Palm Oil (RSPO).

Imagine standing at the edge of a vast plantation. From this vantage point, you see a mosaic of activities: the preparation of the soil, the planting of seeds, and the careful management of resources.

But let's not remain at the periphery; let's dive into the verdant depths to explore each step in detail.

We begin with the land. Choosing the right location is paramount—a place that does not encroach on primary forests or high conservation value areas. The soil whispers secrets of its health, and we must listen, employing soil tests to ensure it is rich in nutrients and free from contaminants. Only then do we proceed to plant seeds that have been genetically selected for their high yield and disease resistance, but not at the cost of biodiversity.

As the young saplings stretch towards the sky, we must nurture them with organic fertilizers and manage pests through biological controls, shunning the harsh pesticides that cause more harm than good. Water, that precious resource, flows through the plantation, but we must use it wisely, employing methods like drip irrigation to reduce wastage.

Our workforce, the guardians of the green, need to be trained in these sustainable practices. They must be well-treated, for their rights and wellbeing are as much a part of sustainability as the health of the trees themselves.

Now, consider for a moment the potential pitfalls. Monocultures ravage the land, stripping it of its multifaceted nature. To avoid this, we introduce intercropping with other beneficial plants, which improves soil health and biodiversity. We remain vigilant against the temptation to expand recklessly, knowing that the land has limits that must be respected.

Once the oil palms have matured, the harvesting of fruit must be done judiciously. We strive for a balance, harvesting enough to meet demand but not so much that it stresses the trees. The mills that extract the oil operate on the principles of zero waste; every byproduct finds a purpose, be it as fertilizer or as raw material for other industries.

How do we know we've succeeded? The validation comes in the form of certification, a seal of approval from third-party organizations that audit our practices against stringent sustainability criteria. The yield of oil is robust, the workers content, the wildlife thrives amidst the plantations, and the carbon footprint is minimized.

But what if problems arise? What if yields fall or pests surge? We turn to experts and research, adapting and evolving our methods. Troubleshooting is an ongoing process, much like the cultivation of the palm tree itself.

Does this seem like an idealistic vision? Perhaps. But it is within our grasp. By following these steps, we tread lightly upon the Earth, leaving a trail of green in our wake. Each drop of palm oil used to power an engine can then be a testament to our dedication to sustainability.

In the end, we circle back to our core mission, our raison d'être: to create a system where palm oil serves not only our functional needs but also honours our profound responsibility to the planet. It's a pursuit that demands our creativity, our passion, and our perseverance.

And so, dear reader, as the sun sets on a sustainable plantation, let us take a moment to bask in the knowledge that each choice we make, each action we take, can contribute to a legacy of sustainability. Let every golden drop of palm oil be a ripple in the vast pond of our collective efforts towards a more sustainable, more hopeful future.

Biodiversity and Ecosystem Health

In the midst of a verdant landscape, where the sun casts its warm embrace upon the earth, lies a truth that is both stark and unsettling. The cultivation of palm oil, as we have seen, can be a beacon of sustainability when practices are carefully orchestrated. Yet, it casts a long shadow over the intricate tapestry of ecosystems where it thrives unchecked. The very essence of our topic, the effects of palm oil production on local ecosystems and biodiversity, is a multifaceted conundrum that demands our utmost attention.

Venture into the heart of a rainforest, and you will be enveloped by a symphony of life—a cacophony of sounds from creatures unseen, a kaleidoscope of green hues, and the earthy scent of life in perpetual motion. Now, imagine that symphony growing fainter, the colors dimming. This is the stark reality we face as palm oil plantations expand, encroaching upon these bastions of biodiversity.

The problem is not one-dimensional; it is the culmination of various factors that erode the very foundation of our natural world. The conversion of rich, diverse forests into monoculture plantations results in a significant loss of flora and fauna. Species endemic to these regions are pushed to the brink of extinction, their habitats replaced by endless rows of oil palm trees. Rhinos, Gorillas, Orangutans, Tigers, and a myriad of other species find their numbers dwindling, their genetic blueprints at risk of being erased from history.

What are the consequences if we turn a blind eye to this growing crisis? The answers whisper through the leaves with a sense of urgency. The loss of biodiversity entails more than just the disappearance of species; it disrupts ecosystems, leading to a cascade of environmental repercussions. Pollination networks falter, soil health degrades, and carbon sequestration capabilities diminish. The very mechanisms that stabilize our climate and sustain life are under threat.

So, what solutions lie at the horizon of this encroaching darkness? The key lies in sustainable development—a path that respects the delicate balance of nature while fulfilling human needs. Initiatives such as the High Carbon Stock (HCS) approach provide a blueprint for identifying vital forest areas that must be preserved. By integrating this with the High Conservation Value (HCV) strategy, we can safeguard areas critical for conserving biodiversity and ecosystems.

Implementing these solutions, however, is akin to nurturing a seedling into a towering tree. It begins with rigorous land analysis, where areas are classified based on their environmental importance. Subsequently, a comprehensive management plan is crafted, delineating zones for protection and sustainable cultivation. It is a delicate dance of give and take, orchestrated with the precision of a master conductor.

The evidence of success whispers through the leaves of those forests that have been saved. In regions where HCS and HCV strategies have been applied, the rebound of biodiversity is palpable. Forests begin to heal, species return, and the land breathes a sigh of relief. These outcomes are not merely anecdotal; they are quantifiable, a testament to the resilience of nature when given a fighting chance.

Yet, are there other ways to thread the needle of conservation and productivity? Certainly, agroforestry emerges as a compelling alternative. By interspersing crops with native vegetation, we can create an agricultural mosaic that supports biodiversity while yielding the precious oil. Another beacon of hope is the push for community-based conservation, where local populations become stewards of the land, empowered to protect their natural heritage.

Is it possible to weave a narrative of conservation that coexists with our quest for palm oil? Can we hold fast to the threads of biodiversity that embroider our world with such rich patterns? The challenge is daunting, yet within it lies the seed of opportunity—an opportunity to redefine our relationship with the natural world, to craft a legacy that future generations will look upon with gratitude.

Let us not forget that every choice we make, every action we take, ripples through the web of life. As the ink dries on these pages, may it serve as a reminder of our collective responsibility—a call to action that resonates with the beating heart of our planet. The time to act is now, for the health of our ecosystems and the wealth of biodiversity they harbor are the ultimate barometers of our success or failure as stewards of this Earth.

Global Warming Potential

In the grand tapestry of human innovation, the quest to harness energy from nature without inflicting harm upon her delicate balance has been a perennial challenge. At the forefront of this quest is the burgeoning industry of biofuels, particularly those derived from palm oil—a golden elixir touted for its potential to power our automobiles with a greener footprint. But does this alternative fuel truly offer an escape from the carbon shackles of traditional fossil fuels, or does it merely masquerade as a solution, while contributing to the very crisis it seeks to avert?

As we delve into the heart of this inquiry, it is imperative to understand the profound impact of palm oil biofuels on global warming. The proposition is clear: palm oil biofuels are often presented as a sustainable alternative to fossil fuels, ostensibly capable of reducing our carbon emissions and mitigating the effects of climate change. Yet, to fully assess the veracity of this claim, one must scrutinize the evidence with an unyielding gaze.

The primary evidence supporting the use of palm oil as a biofuel is its renewable nature. Unlike fossil fuels, which are finite and release carbon that has been sequestered for millennia, biofuels are derived from current biological processes that absorb carbon dioxide during growth. In theory, this creates a closed carbon loop, where the carbon dioxide released during combustion is roughly equal to what was absorbed during the crops' growth phase, resulting in a significantly lower net contribution to global warming.

Delving deeper, studies have shown that palm oil yields are up to nine times higher per hectare than other oilseed crops, suggesting that palm oil could provide a substantial amount of biofuel with less land use. Moreover, proponents argue that with proper management, biofuels from palm oil could reduce greenhouse gas emissions by up to 80% compared to conventional diesel.

However, the narrative takes a complex turn when counter-evidence is considered. Critics of palm oil biofuels point out that the conversion of forests, peatlands, and mangroves into palm oil plantations releases massive amounts of stored carbon, offsetting any potential climate benefits. The process of deforestation and land-use change associated with palm oil cultivation is a significant source of greenhouse gas emissions. In Indonesia and Malaysia, where the majority of palm oil is produced, deforestation and peatland degradation have led to alarmingly high rates of carbon emissions.

In response to these concerns, it is paramount to acknowledge the nuances of the argument. The rebuttal from the biofuel sector emphasizes the development and implementation of sustainable production practices. Certification schemes like the Roundtable on Sustainable Palm Oil (RSPO) are designed to ensure that palm oil is produced without deforestation or the destruction of peatlands, thereby reducing its global warming potential.

Furthermore, additional supporting evidence comes from innovations in agronomy and land management, such as intercropping and improved milling techniques, which can enhance the sustainability of palm oil production. By adopting these practices, the industry strives to minimize its environmental impact and position itself as a true ally in the fight against climate change.

In conclusion, the assertion that palm oil biofuels could play a role in mitigating global warming is one grounded in a vision of sustainable practices and technological advancements. However, this vision must not be viewed through rose-tinted glasses. The stark reality is that without stringent regulations, vigilant enforcement, and a commitment to sustainability, the potential benefits of palm oil biofuels could be eclipsed by the severe consequences of irresponsible land-use changes.

As we stand at the crossroads of environmental stewardship and energy needs, let us ponder a final thought: Can we truly afford to gamble with the delicate equilibrium of our planet for the sake of convenience, or will we rise to the challenge of forging a path that honours the intricate web of life upon which we all depend? The answer to this question will determine the legacy we leave for the Earth and all its inhabitants.

Policy Implications

In the labyrinthine journey towards a more sustainable future, the intersection of environmental policy and the biofuel industry is fraught with contention and complexity. The primary conundrum our book seeks to untangle is whether the pursuit of palm oil as a biofuel is a genuine stride toward eco-friendly transportation or a misguided venture that exacerbates environmental degradation.

The impact of this dilemma is profound, reaching far beyond the sprawling plantations and into the very air we breathe. Imagine a future where the verdant rainforests—once the Earth's lungs—are replaced by unending rows of palm monocultures. This shift not only disturbs biodiversity but also contributes to a cascade of climatic changes. The carbon sequestered in ancient trees and peatlands, released into the atmosphere, accelerates global warming, challenging the very narrative that palm oil as a biofuel reduces our carbon footprint.

To personalize this issue, consider the story of Siti, a smallholder farmer in Indonesia. Her tale is one of transformation; from traditional farming methods to joining a cooperative that promised prosperity through palm oil cultivation. Initially, the profits were substantial, but as time passed, she witnessed the once-rich soil deplete, and the local waterways become lifeless. The monoculture demanded more land, and forests fell to the insatiable appetite of the palm. Siti's dream of progress is now clouded by the smog from forest fires, an annual ritual to clear land for more palm oil plantations. Her narrative is a microcosm of a grander ecological and socio-economic crisis unfolding across the globe.

The stakes could not be higher. If we continue down this path, unchecked and unguided by robust policy, we risk undermining the very foundation of our ecological and climatic systems. We stand at a precipice, where each decision can tip the balance toward recovery or ruin.

However, this book is not just a chronicle of warnings and woes. It is a beacon, guiding us through the tempest toward solutions that acknowledge the intricacies of this issue. It is here we explore how environmental policies, both existing and those yet to be conceived, can shape a sustainable future for palm oil as a biofuel.

How do we craft regulations that safeguard our planet while still nurturing innovation and economic growth? Can certification schemes like the RSPO be enhanced to ensure genuine sustainability? What role do governments play in regulating land-use changes, and can international cooperation amplify these efforts? These are just a few of the critical questions this book will address.

As we delve into the heart of policy implications, we will traverse the landscape of legislation, from local mandates to international agreements. The book deciphers complex regulatory frameworks and distills them into actionable insights that could pivot the industry towards true sustainability.

Imagine a world where policies are not just ink on paper but are enlivened through rigorous enforcement and community engagement. Consider the potential of a future where palm oil plantations coexist with restored forests and where farmers can thrive without sacrificing the environment.

We will investigate the potential of novel agricultural practices that bolster yields without expanding into untouched ecosystems. Technologies that turn waste into wealth will be spotlighted, turning the by-products of palm oil production into energy or materials, thus closing the loop in a truly circular economy.

Moreover, the book will not shy away from the uncomfortable truths. We will confront the economic and political forces that resist change, dissecting their arguments and proposing how policy can be a catalyst for transformation. This journey will not be without its challenges, and this book will serve as a compass, pointing toward the North Star of a balanced and sustainable path forward.

In the chapters that follow, readers will be equipped with knowledge that empowers them to be part of the dialogue. You are invited to question, to critique, and to contribute to the evolving narrative of palm oil as a biofuel.

Will you join us in navigating this complex terrain, where every decision we make today shapes the Earth we bequeath to the generations of tomorrow? The policies we endorse, the practices we implement, and the diligence with which we pursue sustainability will be the legacy of our era. It is a time for bold action and visionary policymaking. Let us embark on this essential quest, with the pages of this book as our map and our collective conscience as the compass.

Chapter Eight

From Local to Global

The Export Journey: Navigating International Markets

The global tapestry of commerce weaves an intricate and dynamic pattern, one that beckons with the promise of growth for those who dare to thread their ambitions across borders. Navigating international markets in the realm of natural oils for automobile power is a journey as challenging as it is rewarding. The goal, then, is straight forward yet substantial: to establish a robust presence in the international oil markets, leveraging the untapped potential of locally sourced natural oils.

Before embarking on this ambitious voyage, let us assemble our navigational tools. The prerequisites for such an endeavour are manifold: a comprehensive understanding of international trade laws, a keen awareness of cultural nuances, a robust supply chain, quality assurance mechanisms, and, not the least, a strategic market entry plan. These are but the cornerstones upon which the edifice of international market presence is built.

A broad overview of the steps involved unfurls before us like a map. It begins with market research and identification, followed by strategic planning, establishing local partnerships, navigating legal and regulatory frameworks, creating a value proposition, and finally, market penetration and growth. This sequential roadmap is our guide through the labyrinth of international trade.

As we delve into the detailed steps, the importance of thorough market research becomes indisputable. One must not only identify potential markets but also understand their complexities. What are the consumer preferences? What is the competition like? How do regulatory landscapes shape the market? Answers to these questions form the bedrock of our strategy.

Upon this foundation, strategic planning takes shape, tailored to each unique market. It is not enough to have a one-size-fits-all approach; adaptability is key. Crafting a bespoke entry strategy that aligns with local customs and consumer behavior is as essential as the oil that powers the engines we aim to fuel.

But what of local partnerships? Herein lies the wisdom of the proverb, "To go fast, go alone. To go far, go together." Local allies can be invaluable, providing insights into the market and facilitating smoother entry. They are the co-navigators in this expedition, helping to steer through unfamiliar waters.

Legal and regulatory frameworks present their own mazes. One must maneuver through these with precision and care, ensuring compliance at every turn. This is not an area for shortcuts; meticulous attention to detail here will prevent setbacks later on.

The value proposition is the banner under which we march into these new territories. What sets our natural oils apart in the global market? Is it their sustainability, their cost-effectiveness, or perhaps their compatibility with a range of automobiles? This unique selling point must resonate with the market's pulse, compelling and persuasive.

Finally, market penetration and growth are the fruits of our labour. It is not enough to simply enter a market; one must also thrive within it. Continuous assessment and adaptation are vital, as is a commitment to innovation and quality. Growth is both the journey and the destination.

Here are some tips and warnings. Do not underestimate the power of cultural intelligence. Missteps in this area can turn potential partners into critics. Beware of overextending in pursuit of rapid expansion; sustainable growth often comes in measured steps. And always, always listen to the market; it speaks volumes to those willing to hear.

How then, do we test or validate our progress? Success metrics vary—from market share growth to brand recognition—but the common denominator is tangible, measurable progress. It is the litmus test that proves our strategies are sound and our efforts fruitful.

Should you encounter obstacles, troubleshooting becomes essential. A common problem is underestimating the time and resources required to establish a presence. To this end, prepare contingency plans, remain flexible in your approach, and keep a keen eye on cash flow and resource allocation.

Navigating international markets is a task that combines the precision of a scientist with the artistry of a poet. It requires a balance of analytical acumen and creative flair. As you forge ahead, remember that the essence of this journey lies in the connection between your product and the people it serves. It is a relationship built on trust, quality, and mutual benefit—a bridge between the local and the global, powered by the very oils you champion.

Competing on the World Stage

In the verdant expanses of Nigeria's lush landscapes, palm trees sway with a hidden promise, their fruits glistening with potential beyond mere nutrition. It is here, amidst the rustling fronds, that we find a treasure poised to reshape the energy landscape—Nigerian palm oil, an unassuming contender in the global arena of automobile power sources. This golden elixir, abundant and renewable, stands at the precipice of a revolution that could see it vying for supremacy with the world's leading oil producers. The question looms: Can Nigerian palm oil compete on the world stage?

To answer this question, we must first understand the key players in this global drama. On one side, we have the traditional titans of the industry, the petroleum giants, whose dominance is rooted in a century of infrastructure, investment, and innovation. On the other, the underdog, Nigerian palm oil, with its sustainable appeal and burgeoning potential. The significance of this comparison lies not in the mere act of juxtaposition but in the unfolding narrative of energy sustainability and the search for renewable resources.

The rationale behind this comparison transcends the academic—it's an urgent inquiry into the future of energy. As the world grapples with the repercussions of climate change and the finite nature of fossil fuels, the spotlight turns to alternatives that can sustain the needs of modern civilization without compromising the health of our planet.

To embark on this exploration, we must establish criteria for a fair and insightful analysis. Yield, environmental impact, cost-effectiveness, and scalability, serve as our benchmarks. These parameters will guide our discourse and enable us to dissect the complexities inherent in each subject.

When we speak of yield, the similarities between both oil sources become apparent. Both petroleum and palm oil are highly energy-dense, capable of delivering a significant amount of power per unit. Yet, it is in their method of extraction and renewability that we begin to see a divergence. Petroleum's extraction is an intensive process, drawing from reserves that are depleting, whereas palm oil offers a more sustainable cycle of production, with trees that bear fruit annually.

This leads us to contrast their environmental impact. The extraction and usage of petroleum have been linked to ecological degradation, from oil spills to greenhouse gas emissions. Palm oil, while not without its issues—deforestation and habitat loss being chief among them—presents an opportunity for a more sustainable approach, one that balances production with environmental stewardship.

Cost-effectiveness, another critical factor, reveals a nuanced picture. Initially, petroleum's established infrastructure and economies of scale give it a pricing advantage. However, as we shift our gaze to the potential of palm oil, the narrative changes. With investment and development, palm oil has the capacity to become not only competitive but also a cost-effective alternative, particularly within local contexts where it can be produced and consumed.

Scalability, the final criterion, is where the challenge and opportunity lie for Nigerian palm oil. The global reliance on petroleum is supported by a colossal, intricate network spanning continents. For palm oil to ascend, it must prove capable of scaling up to meet the demands of a world in motion while maintaining its sustainable edge.

Visual aids, though not present in this text, would serve to crystallize these points, drawing stark lines between the carbon footprint of each oil, the comparative cost over time, and the projected yields under different scenarios of technological advancement.

The insights gleaned from this analysis are profound. Nigerian palm oil, with its inherent renewability and potential for lower environmental impact, possesses the attributes necessary to play a significant role in the future energy mix. It suggests a path forward where energy security and environmental sustainability are not mutually exclusive but can be pursued in tandem.

The contemporary relevance of this comparison is underscored by the current global discourse on energy. Nations are seeking to diversify their energy portfolios, reduce carbon emissions, and adhere to international accords like the Paris Agreement. Nigerian palm oil, if harnessed responsibly, could contribute to these goals, providing a local solution with global ramifications.

In evocative terms, imagine a future where the hum of engines is fueled not by the remnants of prehistoric decay, but by the fruits of trees nurtured under the African sun. It's a future that hinges on foresight, innovation, and the boldness to reimagine the status quo.

What, then, are the broader implications of this burgeoning oil's ascent? Could the up scaling of palm oil production herald a new era of energy independence for developing nations, transforming their landscapes into powerhouses of renewable energy?

As you, the reader, ponder the potential of this green gold, consider the transformative impact it might hold. Envision a world where the roads we travel are lined not with the relics of an oil-dependent past, but with the seeds of a sustainable future, where Nigerian palm oil stands as a testament to what can be achieved when we dare to look beyond the horizon and strive for a balance between progress and preservation.

In Nigeria's quest to compete on the world stage, the journey ahead is undeniably daunting, yet it is paved with possibility. The road winds forward, and on it, the question remains: Will Nigerian palm oil seize its moment in the sun?

Trade Agreements and Barriers

In the intricate dance of global commerce, understanding the intricacies of trade agreements and barriers is not just beneficial; it is imperative, especially when considering the exportation of commodities like palm oil. The flow of this "green gold" across borders is not merely a matter of supply and demand but is intricately tied to a web of regulations and accords that can either facilitate or hinder its journey.

Delving into this complex subject, we encounter terms such as tariffs, subsidies, non-tariff barriers, free trade agreements (FTAs), and economic partnerships. Each of these concepts plays a pivotal role in shaping the destiny of palm oil on the international stage.

Tariffs are taxes imposed on imported goods. They can significantly affect the price competitiveness of palm oil in foreign markets. Subsidies are government financial aid to local producers, cushioning them against international competition, potentially skewing the market in their favor.

Non-tariff barriers are regulations, standards, or procedures that create obstacles to trade. These can range from stringent quality checks to complex administrative processes. Free trade agreements (FTAs) are established between countries to foster trade by reducing or eliminating tariffs and non-tariff barriers. Economic partnerships are broader agreements that may encompass trade but also include investment, aid, and other forms of cooperation.

Each definition unfolds into a broader narrative. Tariffs, for example, can be wielded as tools of economic protectionism, shielding local industries from the tidal waves of global competition. Picture a local farmer, his palms callosed from toil, whose livelihood stands vulnerable to the flood of cheaper, imported goods. Tariffs serve as the barrier protecting not just his income but also the economic landscape of his community.

Subsidies weave their own tale, often controversial, casting shadows of market distortion. They can be seen as lifelines thrown to industries struggling to stay afloat in the competitive sea of international trade. However, critics argue that they can also create unfair advantages, stifle innovation, and lead to trade disputes.

Turning to non-tariff barriers, these can be likened to the complex corridors of a fortress, each turn a new regulation to navigate, each checkpoint a potential delay. For exporters of palm oil, these barriers can be as daunting as physical walls, impeding access to markets that might otherwise be within reach.

Free trade agreements, in contrast, are like grand bridges spanning the chasms between economies, allowing goods to flow more freely. They hold the promise of open markets and expanded horizons, yet they are not without their critics who fear the erosion of local industries and the undermining of labour standards.

Economic partnerships encompass more than just trade; they are the tapestry of international relations, threads of commerce interwoven with strands of diplomacy, aid, and cultural exchange. They represent a holistic approach to economic integration, offering a broader platform for cooperation beyond mere trade.

Do these terms not paint a picture of the global marketplace as a dynamic and sometimes tumultuous ocean, its currents shaped by the winds of policy and agreement? Consider the palm oil exporter, charting a course through these waters, navigating the edges of regulation and the gusts of negotiation to reach the shores of international markets.

But what of the real-world implications of these concepts? Take, for example, the European Union's Renewable Energy Directive, which sets ambitious targets for the use of renewable energy, including biofuels like palm oil. Yet, it also lays down strict sustainability criteria, which can act as non-tariff barriers to entry. Or the African Continental Free Trade Area, a beacon of hope for intra-African trade, which could open new markets for palm oil producers within the continent itself.

As we explore the role of palm oil in powering automobiles, it becomes clear that the journey from oil palm to engine is not a straight path but a route fraught with regulatory twists and turns. The potential for palm oil to be a sustainable energy source is there, but it must navigate the complex map of international trade.

What does the future hold for the export of palm oil in this tangled environment? Will the winds of change bring down the barriers that stand in its way, or will they fortify them, making the path more arduous? It is a critical question, for the answers will shape not only the destiny of palm oil but also the lives of those who depend on its trade.

In the end, we understand that the exportation of palm oil is not just a transaction of goods; it is an intricate ballet of economics, politics, and policy. It is a narrative of aspiration and adversity, a story of how a humble fruit can become a source of power, fueling not only engines but also the engines of international trade. The chapters of this tale are still being written, and its conclusion remains to be seen.

Marketing and Branding Strategies

Amidst the lush greenery of Nigeria's vast plantations, the palm oil industry thrives, a testament to the nation's agricultural prowess and its potential to contribute significantly to the world's renewable energy resources. Yet, despite its promise, Nigerian palm oil remains a hidden gem, its luster obscured by the shadows of international market dynamics and branding challenges.

Enter the scene: the serene backdrop of Nigeria's palm oil farms—rows upon rows of oil palm trees standing as silent sentinels of untapped global potential. The air hums with the sounds of nature, occasionally punctuated by the rhythmic fall of fruit bunches hitting the ground, ready for harvest.

The main players in this narrative are the local farmers and the Nigerian palm oil industry as a whole, supported by a government eager to expand its economic footprint and researchers dedicated to sustainable practices. These entities form a mosaic of ambition and hope, each contributing to the overarching goal of global recognition.

The challenge is clear: How does one elevate a locally abundant, sustainable product to international acclaim? For Nigerian palm oil, the problem is not of quantity or quality but of perception, marketing, and branding on the world stage.

To address this, a robust approach had to be adopted—one that intertwines cultural storytelling with modern marketing techniques. The strategy involved rebranding Nigerian palm oil, not merely as a commodity but as a narrative of heritage, sustainability, and innovation. It was essential to articulate the oil's unique properties, such as its rich red hue, which signifies its high beta-carotene content, and its versatility, which makes it suitable for a wide array of uses, including as a renewable energy source for automobiles.

The results were transformative. By highlighting the oil's sustainable production methods and its role in supporting local communities, the Nigerian palm oil industry begins to gain traction in international markets. Supported by data showing a significant reduction in carbon footprint when utilizing palm oil as biofuel, the narrative began to shift. The product, once overlooked, started to be seen as a frontrunner in the renewable energy sector.

Reflection upon this journey reveals broader insights. It showcases the power of storytelling in marketing—how a narrative that resonates with global consumers can turn the tide in favour of an underdog. This approach, however, is not without its criticisms. Skeptics pointed to the ongoing debates about the environmental impact of palm oil farming, necessitating a continued commitment to sustainable practices and transparency.

Visual aids played a crucial role in this transformation. Info graphics depicting the sustainable farming practices, charts illustrating the carbon emissions comparison between palm oil biofuels and fossil fuels, and captivating images of the vibrant local communities all served to demystify the product and engage the audience on an emotional level.

The case of Nigerian palm oil is not an isolated tale. It connects to the larger narrative of how developing countries can leverage their natural resources to compete in a global economy increasingly concerned with sustainability and ethical sourcing.

But what of the future? Will the strategies employed to elevate Nigerian palm oil's status on the world stage pave the way for other such products? Can the lessons learned here be a blueprint for similar marketing endeavours?

Rockson Rapu, an entrepreneur and award-winning author, a business consultant, and a mentor to the next generation, posits that the intersection of cultural heritage and modern marketing is fertile ground for innovation. The Nigerian palm oil case study stands as a beacon to other industries seeking to harness their local resources for global impact.

One must ponder, then: What other natural treasures lie dormant within the soils of our world's diverse landscapes, waiting for the right combination of storytelling and strategy to propel them into the limelight?

In a world that thirsts for sustainability and authenticity, the tale of Nigerian palm oil is a reminder that sometimes, the most potent fuel for progress is the story we choose to tell.

Success Stories of Export

Beneath the relentless sun, the port of Lagos buzzed with an energy that could rival that of the sun itself. Men shouted orders over the din of machinery while cranes hoisted containers painted with the green and white of Nigeria. Among these containers, a special batch—marked with the insignia of a rising sun—held within its steel walls a cargo of liquid gold: refined palm oil, destined for shores far beyond the African continent.

This scene was the culmination of a vision held by Akin Afolabi, a man whose name had become synonymous with the palm oil export renaissance in Nigeria. Afolabi wasn't just another entrepreneur; he was a visionary, a man who saw the potential in the red rivers that flowed from the oil palms of his homeland.

His story began in the humble groves of his family's farm, where as a boy, he learned the secrets of the oil palms from his grandfather, a man whose hands were as gnarled as the trees he tended but whose eyes shone with the wisdom of the land. It was these lessons that rooted the young Afolabi in the belief that the oil from these trees could fuel not just the lanterns of his village but the engines of the world.

Years of research and experimentation had led him to a breakthrough that could turn the tide for Nigerian palm oil. He had discovered a way to refine the oil to meet the stringent standards required for use in automobiles—a revelation that promised to transform the industry.

Afolabi's journey was not without its trials. He faced skepticism from those who could not envision palm oil beyond the kitchen. He weathered the storms of fluctuating markets and the gales of international trade policies. Yet, with every challenge, his resolve only strengthened, much like the oil palms that weathered the seasonal rains.

The emotional landscape of our protagonist was a tapestry of determination, fear, and hope. Afolabi had risked everything on this venture. His heart raced as he watched the containers being loaded onto the ship. This was more than a personal triumph; it was a beacon of possibility for his country.

As the ship set sail, it carried with it not only palm oil but the dreams of a nation. It was a surprising turn, a narrative once confined to the local markets now stretching across oceans. The world was about to witness the versatility of Nigerian palm oil, not just as a culinary ingredient but as a sustainable energy source.

This unexpected journey mirrored the unpredictable nature of the book's subject—how natural oils, often overlooked, could power the future. It spoke to the universal truth that innovation and tradition could coexist, that the roots of progress might lie in the very soil we stand upon.

Akin Afolabi's success story was a testament to the wisdom that when harnessed correctly, local resources like palm oil could not only empower a nation but also make a global impact. The palm oil that once lit the homes of his village had the potential to light the way to a greener future for the automotive industry.

What lessons can be gleaned from this tale? How can other nations replicate this model of local resource to global triumph? These were the questions that stirred in the minds of readers, promising insights into the transformative power of vision, innovation, and the indomitable human spirit.

As Rockson Rapu penned these words, he was reminded of the journey he chronicled in "Waking up the Troubled Giant" and "Saving Her from Jezebel." It is the same spirit of enterprise and resilience that courses through the veins of this narrative. As a business consultant, he has always believed in the power of stories to inspire change and spur action.

So, let us ask ourselves: What untapped resources lie in our backyards, waiting for the spark of ingenuity to ignite them? How many more Akin Afolabis are out there, holding the keys to the next revolution in renewable energy?

In a world where the demand for sustainable solutions grows daily, the story of Nigerian palm oil is not just a success to be celebrated but a promise of what is possible when we look to nature for our inspiration. It is a narrative that beckons us to explore the riches that lie within our reach, to seek out the oil that can fuel not just our engines but our collective imagination.

Chapter Nine

The Socio-Economic Ripple Effect

Job Creation and Employment

In the verdant landscapes of tropical regions, where the sky kisses the earth at every sunset, lie fields of gold—palm oil plantations stretching as far as the eye can see. Here, in this serene backdrop, begins a story not just of agriculture and industry, but of human lives and their relentless quest for sustenance and prosperity.

The main players in this narrative are the local farmers, the mill operators, the transporters, and the array of ancillary service providers. Each with a story etched on their palms, worn by labour yet uplifted by the hope of a better future. They are the backbone of the palm oil industry, an industry that has been both lauded for its economic potential and scrutinized for its environmental impact.

The challenge at the heart of this case study is multifaceted. There's the pressing issue of unemployment in rural areas, the need for sustainable development, and the global demand for alternative energy sources. The palm oil industry stands at this crossroad, holding in its grasp the power to mold these challenges into avenues for employment and growth.

The approach adopted by these communities was strategic and multifaceted. They leveraged the local abundance of palm oil to create a vertically integrated model that spans from cultivation to processing, refining, and ultimately the production of biofuel. This model not only maximizes the use of each part of the palm but also generates a variety of job roles, from agricultural technicians to mechanical engineers.

The results were nothing short of transformative. The introduction of palm oil biofuel production led to a significant uptick in local employment. For instance, in one community, the employment rate soared by 30% within the first two years of adopting this model. Smallholder farmers, once struggling to find markets for their produce, now had a steady demand. Mill operators expanded their workforce to meet production needs, while logistics companies flourished, transporting goods to international markets.

However, this success story is not without its criticisms. There are voices that point to the environmental risks associated with palm oil cultivation—deforestation and loss of biodiversity being at the forefront. Reflecting on this, it becomes evident that while the industry has been a boon for job creation, it must tread carefully to balance economic benefits with ecological preservation.

Graphs and charts, depicting the skyrocketing employment rates and the subsequent rise in local economies, serve as visual aids to underscore the profound impact of this industry.

This case study is a microcosm of the larger narrative of 'Oil to Function,' illustrating how local resources, when harnessed sustainably, can power not just automobiles but also the engines of community growth and development. And so if the palm oil industry can stimulate such profound economic change, what potential lies untapped in other natural resources? How can we, as a society, work towards unlocking this potential in a way that honours the earth and its inhabitants?

In this journey of exploration, Rockson Rapu invites you to consider the possibilities. As we continue to mentor the next generation, let us impart the wisdom of sustainable prosperity and the courage to innovate for the greater good. Join in envisioning a future where natural oils not only power our vehicles but also fuel the aspirations of people across the globe.

Community Development

In the embrace of dawn, a community awakens to the sound of machinery and the scent of progress. Palm trees, swaying gently in the morning breeze, are more than just a feature of the landscape—they are pillars of a burgeoning industry that promises to enrich lives and elevate societies from the clutches of poverty. The palm oil industry, an emblem of opportunity, has become a catalyst for profound community development.

Beneath the verdant canopy of oil palm plantations, the narrative unfolds of how a simple, natural resource can be the keystone for collective prosperity. This chapter in our journey—'Oil to Function'—is not merely about mechanized revolutions but about the human spirit, the community heartbeat that finds its rhythm in the extraction and refinement of palm oil.

At the core of this discourse lies a bold assertion: the palm oil industry has the potential to foster community development and improve living standards in a tangible, long-lasting manner. It's a proposition that demands scrutiny, supported by the tangible outcomes observed in regions where palm oil production is intertwined with daily life.

The primary evidence for this claim originates from the economic stimulation that follows the establishment of palm oil operations. In regions like Southeast Asia and parts of Africa, the cultivation and processing of palm oil have led to the creation of job opportunities in areas where employment was once scarce. From the planting of the trees to the intricate refining processes, each step in the palm oil supply chain has opened doors to livelihoods that were previously unattainable.

Yet, to delve deeper into the evidence, one must look beyond the numbers. The rise in employment is accompanied by an increase in local spending power. Small businesses flourish, educational facilities receive better funding, and healthcare services improve as a direct consequence of the industry's financial contributions to the community.

However, the sheen of progress is not without its blemishes. Detractors of the palm oil narrative point to the potential for exploitation, both of the environment and labour. Deforestation and the displacement of indigenous communities are stark realities that cannot be ignored. Moreover, the concern of fair wages and working conditions for labourers casts a long shadow over the industry's purported benefits.

In response to such concerns, a nuanced rebuttal emerges: sustainability and ethical practices are becoming the cornerstones of modern palm oil production. Certification schemes like the Roundtable on Sustainable Palm Oil (RSPO) ensure that member companies adhere to strict guidelines that prioritize environmental conservation and social responsibility. These mechanisms work to counterbalance the industry's negative aspects and highlight its commitment to continual improvement.

Beyond the primary evidence and its challenges, additional support for the industry's positive role in community development comes from educational advancements. Scholarships and training programs funded by palm oil profits have enabled countless individuals to pursue higher education, thus fostering a more skilled workforce. This, in turn, leads to innovation and the potential for diversification within the industry, such as the development of palm oil-based biofuels that promise a cleaner, renewable energy source for the future.

Drawing this exploration to a close, the reinforced assertion stands clear: the palm oil industry, when conducted with conscientious attention to sustainability and ethics, has the power to transform communities. The evidence—economic growth, improved infrastructure, and educational opportunities—underscores a story of progress written in the language of shared success.

The horizon of possibility stretches out, inviting us to imagine a world where the fruits of the earth are harvested not just for their material yield but for the harvest of human potential they yield. Could the palm oil industry be the template upon which other natural resource sectors build their own narratives of community development and social elevation?

It is here, amid the whispers of palm fronds, that we ponder the profound implications of our relationship with nature's bounty. How we choose to engage with it will define not only the future of our automobiles but the very fabric of our societies. Let us steer this course with wisdom, for in the oil that lubricates our engines may well lie the elixir for a thriving global community.

Women and Youth Empowerment

In the heart of Nigeria, where the sun casts a relentless glow over verdant fields, a revolution is underway—a revolution not of conflict, but of empowerment and prosperity. Here, amid the sprawling plantations of oil palms, a narrative is being woven, one that tells of women and the youth stepping into roles that reshape their destinies and the economic fabric of their communities.

The palm oil industry in Nigeria has long been a cornerstone of the economy, but its potential to empower the historically marginalized segments of society is only now being brought into sharp focus. The issue at hand is clear: while palm oil production has contributed significantly to the nation's GDP, the benefits have not always trickled down to those who toil upon the land—particularly women and the youth.

What then, one might ask, are the consequences of leaving this potential untapped? The stark reality is that without active involvement in lucrative industries such as palm oil production, these groups may remain ensnared in the vicious cycle of poverty. The absence of empowerment leads to social stagnation, where talents are wasted, and aspirations are quelled before they can even take flight.

But within this challenge lies an opportunity—a chance to rewrite the narrative. Empowerment through the palm oil industry can be achieved by adopting a more inclusive approach to employment and entrepreneurship within the sector. Women and the youth can be trained and given the means to engage in the production, processing, and marketing of palm oil. Such initiatives could serve as a beacon of hope, illuminating a path to financial independence and societal contribution.

Implementing such a vision requires a multilayered approach. First, education and training programs must be established to provide the necessary skills to excel in the industry. These programs would cover topics such as sustainable farming practices, business management, and the mechanics of the global palm oil market.

Following the educational phase, microfinance opportunities should be made available to enable women and the youth to start their own palm oil-related ventures or to improve existing operations. By equipping them with both knowledge and capital, we set the stage for a more equitable and dynamic industry.

The evidence of success from such interventions is not merely theoretical. Take, for example, the initiatives in other regions where similar empowerment programs have led to increased household incomes, higher levels of education among children, and a palpable sense of autonomy among women. In these success stories, the ripple effects are clear: communities thrive, economies grow, and the quality of life improves.

What if, however, such top-down approaches are not feasible or sufficient? Alternative solutions might include grassroots movements that advocate for land rights, fair pay, and representation of women and the youth in the decision-making structures of the palm oil industry. These movements can generate a coalition of change, ensuring that empowerment is not just a gift bestowed from above but a right claimed by those who seek it.

One cannot help but wonder, how will the landscape of Nigeria's palm oil industry transform if these solutions are embraced? Can you envision a future where the industry not only fuels automobiles but also the dreams and ambitions of its people? The prospect is tantalizing—a future where the wealth generated by natural resources is equitably shared, creating a more robust and resilient society.

Herein lies the essence of our quest for empowerment within the palm oil narrative. It's not just about elevating the lives of individuals; it's about cultivating a community that thrives on the principles of inclusivity and sustainability. As the pages of this story unfold, let us not be mere spectators. Let us be the scribes who, through deliberate action and unwavering commitment, inscribe a new chapter for the women and the youth of Nigeria—one where their roles in the palm oil industry become a testament to their strength, their contribution, and their unyielding hope for a brighter tomorrow.

Economic Diversification

In the tapestry of Nigerian economic history, threads of green and black have been interwoven to create a vibrant, yet at times, volatile picture. Travel back in time, and one discovers a Nigeria where agriculture was the country's lifeline, the verdant green of palm oil plantations symbolising prosperity and sustenance. However, as the black gold - crude oil - gushed from the Niger Delta, the nation's focus shifted, luring it into a decades-long dependence that has shaped its economy and global standing.

Historically, Nigeria's economic narrative took a dramatic turn in the late 1950s when crude oil was first discovered. The subsequent oil boom of the 1970s transformed the country into a petro-state, with revenues from oil exports flooding the national coffers. This influx led to a decline in other sectors, particularly agriculture. The once-thriving palm oil industry, which had been a significant export product, was eclipsed by the allure of this newfound wealth.

From past to present, the consequences of this shift have been profound. The reliance on oil has made Nigeria's economy susceptible to the whims of global oil prices, leading to a cyclical pattern of booms and busts. This pattern in oil price booms and bursts now underscore the urgency for economic diversification to create a more stable and resilient economy.

Why does this history matter now? Understanding the past provides insight into the challenges that Nigeria faces today. The over-reliance on oil has not only made the economy vulnerable but also stifled innovation and growth in other sectors. By revisiting the agricultural roots, particularly through the lens of palm oil, Nigeria can tap into a sustainable and lucrative industry that has the potential to empower local communities and drive economic growth.

Can you imagine a future where Nigeria's economy is no longer at the mercy of volatile oil prices? Where the value of green gold - palm oil - is recognized not only for its culinary uses but also for its potential in powering automobiles? This is the contemporary exploration that "Oil to Function" undertakes. It is a story of renaissance, resilience, and reinvention.

In the quest for economic diversification, palm oil presents a compelling case. It is an industry that has the potential to stimulate rural development, create jobs, and generate income for millions. Nigeria, blessed with a climate conducive to oil palm cultivation, could once again take its place as a leading producer, a position it held before the oil boom. The role of palm oil in this new chapter of Nigeria's economy cannot be overstated.

The path to diversification is not without obstacles. Challenges such as land rights, access to finance, and the need for modernization of farming techniques loom large. Yet, the potential rewards beckon—a more stable economy, improved livelihoods for rural farmers, and a reduction in environmental degradation as a result of sustainable agricultural practices.

The question that remains is not whether palm oil can help diversify the Nigerian economy, but rather how quickly and effectively the necessary changes can be implemented. Will the government and the private sector rise to the occasion, providing the support and infrastructure needed to revitalize this industry? Will the local farmers be empowered through access to education, technology, and markets to ensure that the benefits of growth are widely shared?

One-line paragraph for emphasis:

The time for change is now.

Incorporating direct questions, let us ponder: How will Nigeria navigate the complex journey of economic diversification? Will it reclaim its legacy as an agricultural powerhouse, harnessing the potential of palm oil to fuel not just vehicles, but also its economy?

As we delve deeper into the pages of "Oil to Function," we are reminded that every drop of oil, be it from the fruit of a palm or the depth of the earth, carries with it the power to transform. In Nigeria's hands lies the opportunity to channel this power not merely into the engines of automobiles but into the engine of the economy itself. The story of palm oil is not one of nostalgia; it is a narrative of possibility, a call to action, and a roadmap to a future where the wealth of the land is matched by the wealth of its people.

International Relations and Diplomacy

In the dense tapestry of international trade, the vibrant hues of palm oil have painted Nigeria's diplomatic canvas with strokes of ingenuity and necessity. This liquid treasure, once the backbone of the nation's agrarian economy, has re-emerged as a pivotal actor in Nigeria's quest for economic diversification and sustainability, redefining its engagement on the world stage.

In the realm of international relations and diplomacy, the palm oil trade has become Nigeria's olive branch, extended to the world in an offering of partnership and progress. It's a narrative that's as much about the oil as it is about the hands that cultivate it, and the bonds that are strengthened or strained in its trade.

By incorporating the occasional one-liner for emphasis, direct questions to provoke thought, and a meticulous attention to rhythm and cadence, Rockson Rapu crafts a compelling case study in "Oil to Function: Pioneering Campaign for Biofuels as Alternative Energy Solution." It's a book that not only informs but also inspires, urging the reader to contemplate the transformative power of what might seem, at first glance, to be the most ordinary of commodities.

In conclusion, Rockson Rapu leaves the reader with a resonant thought: As we harness the gifts of nature to fuel our machines, might we also fuel a brighter future for our nations? This, perhaps, is the greatest power of the humble palm oil, and the ultimate challenge for Nigeria's place in the global community.

Chapter Ten

The Future of Oil:
Innovations and Predictions: Technological Breakthroughs

In a world teetering on the cusp of energy transformation, the advent of technologies capable of harnessing natural oils for automotive energy is not just an aspiration but a burgeoning reality. The quest for sustainable fuel sources has led us to the doorstep of innovation, where the once humble oils derived from local flora are poised to power the engines of tomorrow. This chapter is dedicated to the emerging technologies that could revolutionize the production and use of natural oils, setting the stage for an eco-friendly paradigm shift in the automobile industry.

As we stand at the threshold of this green revolution, it is crucial to recognize the key innovations that serve as the pillars of this transition.

1. Enzymatic Biodiesel Conversion

2. Solar-Powered Oil Extraction

3. Nano-Catalysis for Oil Refinement

4. Genetic Engineering of Oil-Producing Crops

5. Advanced Biofuel Cells

Each of these points will be dissected, revealing the intricacies of their functions, the evidence of their potential, and the practicality of their application in the real world.

Enzymatic Biodiesel Conversion

The first technological marvel is the enzymatic conversion process for producing biodiesel. Unlike conventional methods that rely on chemical processes requiring high temperatures and pressures, enzymatic conversion operates at the molecular level. Enzymes, nature's catalysts, are employed to break down the oil molecules, esterifying or trans-esterifying them into fatty acid methyl esters – the chemical constituents of biodiesel. This breakthrough offers a gentler, more energy-efficient method of fuel production.

Researchers around the globe have documented substantial reductions in waste and energy consumption with this technology. An example that stands out is a study conducted by the University of Porto, which achieved a 90% conversion efficiency using enzymatic processes. Testimonials from industry experts highlight the process's lower toxicity and reduced environmental impact compared to traditional methods.

In practice, this technology can be seamlessly integrated into existing biodiesel production facilities, requiring only the addition of enzyme reactors. It paves the way for smaller, localized production units that can operate closer to the source of natural oils, reducing transportation costs and carbon emissions.

Solar-Powered Oil Extraction

Imagine fields of sunflowers not just turning their faces to the sun but also harnessing its energy to extract the very oil within their seeds. This is not a mere flight of fancy; solar-powered oil extraction is turning this vision into reality. By leveraging photovoltaic cells, the energy-intensive process of oil extraction is being reimagined. Solar power drives the mechanical presses or solvent-based extractors, significantly cutting down the reliance on fossil fuels.

The implications are staggering. A pilot project in a remote village in India demonstrated that using solar power for oil extraction could reduce energy costs by up to 70%. With the sun as an ally, the process of extracting oil becomes cleaner, more sustainable, and infinitely more accessible to communities far removed from the electrical grid.

Nano-Catalysis for Oil Refinement

On the forefront of material science, nano-catalysts are rewriting the rules of oil refinement. These microscopic marvels are designed to increase the surface area for chemical reactions, thus accelerating the process and enhancing the efficiency of turning crude natural oils into fuel-grade material.

One compelling piece of evidence comes from a study published in the journal Nature, which reported a 50% increase in catalytic activity using nano-scale catalysts. These enhancements mean that less energy is required, and the refinement can occur at lower temperatures, reducing the carbon footprint of the entire process.

The practicality of nano-catalysis lies in its adaptability. Existing refineries can be retrofitted with nano-catalysts, allowing them to reap the benefits of this technology without a complete overhaul of their infrastructure.

Genetic Engineering of Oil-Producing Crops

Genetic engineering stands at the vanguard of agricultural technology, and when applied to oil-producing crops, it holds the promise of dramatically increased yields and the potential to engineer plants that can thrive in suboptimal conditions. By manipulating the genetic makeup of these plants, scientists are creating varieties with higher oil content and resistance to pests and diseases.

A striking example lies in the development of a genetically modified canola plant that produces oil with a composition more suitable for biodiesel production. Field trials have shown a 20% increase in oil yield per acre compared to traditional varieties.

Advanced Biofuel Cells

Lastly, we delve into the realm of biofuel cells, devices that directly convert the energy stored in natural oils into electricity. These cells operate on the principles of bio-electro-catalysis, using enzymes or microorganisms to break down the oil molecules, releasing electrons that can be harnessed as electrical power. Advanced biofuel cells promise a cleaner, more efficient way to power electric vehicles, with the tantalizing prospect of refueling with liquid oils.

A study from the Massachusetts Institute of Technology has showcased a prototype biofuel cell with an energy conversion efficiency that rivals that of traditional fuel cells. In a world increasingly leaning towards electric vehicles, the application of such technology could provide a bridge between liquid fuels and electric power, offering a versatile and eco-friendly solution.

As we explore these technological breakthroughs, one question looms large: how soon will we witness their integration into our daily lives, reshaping the way we think about fuel and energy? The answer lies not just in the laboratories and test fields but in the collective will to adopt and invest in these technologies for a cleaner, more sustainable future.

With each step forward, we move closer to a world where automobiles are powered by the very essence of the earth's flora, their engines humming a tune of harmony with nature. It is a vision both inspiring and attainable, and as we turn the page on traditional fuels, we may soon find ourselves gliding down highways lined with the verdant fields of our fuel's origin. The road ahead is bright, and it is paved with the golden promise of natural oils.

Chapter Eleven

Market Dynamics and Trends

The evolving landscape of the automobile industry, with its shifting gears towards sustainability and renewable energy sources, paints an intriguing picture of the future of natural oils in powering our vehicles. The market for natural oils as biofuels is poised on a precipice, ready to soar on the wings of environmental consciousness and technological prowess. But what drives this market, and how will the relentless forces of supply and demand, innovation, and regulation influence the trajectory of these green fuels? This chapter delves into the predictive analysis of market dynamics and trends, forecasting the role of natural oils in the automotive realm.

The central theme of this discourse hinges on the proposition that the increasing demand for environmentally friendly alternatives to fossil fuels, coupled with advancements in technology and supportive regulatory frameworks, will significantly bolster the market for natural oils in the automotive industry. To understand this assertion, we must first examine the primary evidence that feeds this claim.

A glaring piece of evidence lies in the rising global concerns over climate change and the urgent call for action to reduce greenhouse gas emissions. The Paris Agreement, a landmark accord adopted by nearly every nation in 2015, underscores a collective drive towards curbing the reliance on fossil fuels. This global commitment is a catalyst for change, inciting governments and industries alike to seek out renewable alternatives, including natural oils for automotive use.

The data supporting this trend is compelling. The International Energy Agency (IEA) reports a steady increase in the investment and use of biofuels, with natural oils gaining significant attention due to their lower carbon footprint compared to traditional fuels. Moreover, recent market analysis projects that the biofuel sector will grow at a compound annual growth rate of approximately 5% over the next decade, with vegetable oil-based fuels expected to occupy a substantial portion of this growth.

Digging deeper, one cannot overlook the innovation in agricultural practices and genetic engineering that has vastly improved the yield and quality of oil-producing crops. For instance, the enhanced canola varieties, which boast a higher oil content suitable for biodiesel production, are a testament to the potential scalability of natural oil production. Such developments diminish the concerns about meeting the increasing demand for biofuels without compromising food security or biodiversity.

However, the narrative is not without its counterarguments. Critics point to the limited availability of arable land and the food versus fuel debate, warning that the large-scale production of biofuels could lead to deforestation and threaten food crop cultivation. Furthermore, there are skeptics who question the energy efficiency of biofuel production and the true environmental impact when considering the entire lifecycle of these fuels.

In response to these counterarguments, it is essential to highlight the ongoing research and development in the field of biofuels. Innovations such as enzymatic biodiesel conversion and solar-powered oil extraction are transforming the production process, making it more energy-efficient and less reliant on arable land. Additionally, regulatory frameworks are being put in place to ensure sustainable practices, such as the European Union's Renewable Energy Directive, which mandates the use of land with low biodiversity or low carbon stock for biofuel crop cultivation.

Augmenting the discourse with additional evidence, industry giants in the automotive sector are beginning to embrace natural oil-based fuels. Partnerships between biofuel producers and car manufacturers are on the rise, with some companies already offering vehicles compatible with biodiesel blends. These collaborations signal a growing confidence in the viability of natural oils as a mainstream fuel alternative.

In conclusion, the assertion that natural oils will play a pivotal role in the future of automotive fuels is underpinned by a robust foundation of environmental imperatives, technological advances, and strategic market positioning. The demand for sustainable and clean energy sources is not a fleeting trend but a fundamental shift in the global energy paradigm. As we continue to witness the embrace of natural oils in powering automobiles, the market dynamics suggest a future where the hum of engines harmonizes with the rustle of leaves — a future driven by the essence of the earth's flora, refined by human ingenuity, and governed by the responsible stewardship of our planet. The road ahead for natural oils is not just bright; it is transformative, and it beckons with open arms.

Chapter Twelve

Policy and Regulation Forecast

In the midst of a rapidly evolving energy landscape, the natural oil industry stands at the forefront of a significant revolution. This chapter delves into the anticipated policy and regulatory changes that could shape the future of this burgeoning sector. As the world tilts its axis towards renewable energy sources, the implications for natural oils, particularly in powering automobiles, are profound. But what challenges lie ahead, and how might the industry navigate the complex web of future governance?

The current issue at hand is the dichotomy between the need for rapid expansion of the natural oil industry to meet environmental targets and the existing regulatory frameworks that were primarily designed for a fossil fuel-dependent world. This misalignment presents a primary challenge, as outdated policies could stifle innovation and growth within the natural oil sector.

Should this problem go unaddressed, the consequences could range from missed opportunities in reducing carbon emissions to a failure in achieving energy independence. The potential stagnation of the natural oil industry's growth could also lead to economic losses, particularly in regions ripe for the cultivation and processing of oil-producing crops.

The solution lies in the formulation and implementation of forward-thinking policies that are specifically tailored to nurture and accelerate the adoption of natural oils as a viable alternative to traditional automotive fuels. This would involve a multi-pronged approach, incorporating incentives for research and development, subsidies for farmers, and the establishment of standards and certifications for natural oil products.

To put this solution into action, a sequence of steps must be undertaken. Firstly, governments must engage with industry experts and stakeholders to gain insights into the specific needs of the natural oil market. This collaboration would inform the creation of targeted policies that address the unique challenges and opportunities within the sector. Subsequent steps would include the drafting of legislation, public consultation, and finally, the enactment of laws that provide a stable and supportive environment for the industry to flourish.

Evidence of such policies' efficacy can be drawn from analogous scenarios. For instance, the solar energy industry saw exponential growth following the implementation of government incentives and supportive regulations. Tax credits, rebates, and feed-in tariffs have proven instrumental in propelling the solar market forward. Similarly, for natural oils, tailored policies could ignite a comparable surge in industry expansion and technological advancements.

While the proposed solution appears promising, it is critical to consider alternative solutions. These might include voluntary industry-led initiatives to standardize and promote natural oils or international agreements that encourage cross-border cooperation in the development of a global natural oil market. Each alternative must be weighed for its potential impact and feasibility in the context of a diverse and multifaceted energy sector.

What if the industry were to hinge solely on market forces, without the guiding hand of policy? Would the invisible hand be enough to steer the market towards sustainability? These direct questions challenge us to ponder the role of governance in shaping an industry that is not only commercially viable but also environmentally imperative.

To paint a more vivid picture, imagine a world where the scent of fresh canola and sunflower fields blends with the purring of engines on the highway. This is a world where policies have paved the way for innovation, green energy, and economic growth. It is a world where the once-clear line between agriculture and automotive industries has been blurred to create a synergetic force for good.

In summary, the natural oil industry sits on the cusp of a major transition, with policies and regulations playing a pivotal role in determining its trajectory. The forecast is clear: change is imminent, and it behooves us to ensure that the shift is in favour of a sustainable and prosperous future. As we look ahead, let us remember that the journey from Oil to function is not just about fueling cars; it is about fueling change.

Chapter Thirteen

Cultural Shifts and Consumer Behaviour

As dawn breaks over the lush landscapes of our agricultural heartlands, a new era is quietly unfolding. Here, amid the rustle of green leaves, lies the pulse of an emerging revolution. This is where tradition meets innovation, where cultural shifts and consumer behavior are beginning to drive the adoption of natural oils in powering automobiles.

Picture a small community, once reliant solely on conventional farming, now at the forefront of this change. They have ventured into the cultivation of oil-rich crops, spurred on by a collective vision of a cleaner, more sustainable future. This isn't just a tale of environmental stewardship; it's a narrative of resilience and adaptation.

Within this microcosm, the main players are the local farmers, the innovative entrepreneurs, and the environmentally conscious consumers. The farmers, guardians of the soil, have generations of agricultural wisdom encoded in their practices. Yet, they find themselves at a crossroads, challenged by the need to adapt to a market hungry for sustainable energy sources. Entrepreneurs, armed with a blend of business acumen and technological savvy, seek to bridge the gap between tradition and progress. Meanwhile, consumers, increasingly aware of their ecological footprint, demand products that align with their values.

The challenge, stark and daunting, is the inertia of old habits and the skepticism surrounding alternative energy sources. How does one convince a society weaned on fossil fuels that the future lies in the fields they pass by every day?

The approach was multifaceted. The farmers were introduced to new agronomic techniques that maximized the yield of oil-producing crops. Entrepreneurs launched campaigns to educate the community about the benefits of natural oils, not just as a sustainable choice but also as a financially viable one. Workshops and seminars became the crucibles where skepticism melted into curiosity and interest.

Results began to surface like seedlings in fertile ground. Farmers reported higher profits and a renewed sense of purpose. Entrepreneurs witnessed the growth of a new market niche. Consumers reveled in the knowledge that their choices contributed to a greener planet. Data, the unwavering witness, showed a marked reduction in carbon emissions within the community, an inspiring testament to the potential of this initiative.

Reflecting on this case study, one cannot ignore the broader implications. It is a microcosm that mirrors the macrocosm of global potential. Of course, there were criticisms—concerns about the scalability of such projects and the true environmental impact when considering the entire lifecycle of natural oils. Yet, these dialogues only served to fuel further innovation and refinement of the approach.

Visual aids, such as before-and-after photographs of the transformed farmlands and info-graphics displaying emission reductions, painted a compelling picture of the transformation. These images were not just proofs of concept but invitations to imagine a different world.

Tying back to the larger narrative, this case study is a single thread in the vast tapestry of cultural evolution. It shows how local endeavors can ripple outward, influencing consumer behavior and, ultimately, effecting global change.

So, as we stand at this crossroads, let us pose a vital question: What if every community took a leaf from this book? Imagine the collective impact, the symphony of engines humming in harmony with the environment. Could this be the tipping point for a worldwide shift towards sustainability?

In the end, the story of natural oils is not just about alternative energy—it is about a cultural metamorphosis. It is about recognizing the power of our choices, both as producers and consumers, and the indelible mark they leave on the world. As an entrepreneur, author, and mentor, Rockson Rapu has witnessed the profound capacity of human ingenuity and spirit. Now, as we face the horizon of a new dawn, let us step forward with the courage to embrace change and the wisdom to sustain it.

Chapter Fourteen

Scenarios for Sustainable Growth

In the shadows of what was once an unyielding reliance on fossil fuels, a new chapter is being penned. This narrative is not of scarcity or fear, but of abundance and foresight—where the natural oil sector emerges as a protagonist in the tale of sustainable growth. We find ourselves at a juncture where the demand for cleaner energy is not just a whisper in the winds of change but a clarion call that resonates across continents.

Imagine a world where the streets no longer reek of petrol but are instead graced with the subtle, earthy scent of natural oils. This is a realm where engines roar to life, powered by the very essence of the soil. The current issue at hand is not the lack of technology or resources but the inertia of transition from the old guard of energy to the new.

The burgeoning natural oil industry stands poised, ready to break the shackles of traditional fuel sources. Yet, for every stride it takes, it confronts the specter of entrenched systems and economic structures that favour the status quo. This is the canvas upon which we must paint our vision for the future—a tapestry of green energy interwoven with the threads of sustainability and innovation.

The crux of our dilemma lies in the scalability of natural oils as a viable alternative to fossil fuels. Can the cultivation of oil-rich crops keep pace with the voracious appetite of the global automobile industry? How do we reconcile the need for land to grow these crops with the necessity to preserve natural habitats and ensure food security?

Should we falter in our quest, the consequences are not merely inconvenient but potentially catastrophic. Imagine the suffocating blanket of pollution tightening its grip on our cities, the relentless march of climate change hastening the extinction of countless species—ours included. We face a world where geopolitical tensions escalate as nations scramble for the last drops of a dwindling resource.

Yet, within this brewing storm, we find our beacon of hope. The solution lies in the heart of innovation and the spirit of collaboration. We propose a multifaceted approach that includes the development of high-yield, low-impact oil crops, the advancement of oil extraction and processing technologies, and the creation of robust economic models that incentivize the switch to natural oils.

The journey begins with the seed—the literal and figurative embodiment of potential. Scientists and agronomists must work hand in hand to engineer crops that thrive in a variety of climates, resisting pests and yielding abundant oil. Concurrently, we must refine the methods of oil extraction to increase efficiency and reduce waste.

Next, comes the cultivation of a symbiotic relationship between farmers and the automobile industry. Through fair-trade agreements and subsidies, we can ensure that the farmers who nurture these crops are justly rewarded, fostering an environment where sustainability is not just ecologically sound but economically viable.

Evidence of success is not merely anecdotal; it is quantifiable. Pilot programs in diverse regions have demonstrated that vehicles powered by natural oils can reduce carbon emissions by up to 85% compared to their petroleum-guzzling counterparts. Predictive models suggest that with full-scale adoption, the natural oil sector could generate millions of jobs worldwide, invigorating the local economies and contributing to a greener planet.

Some naysayers advocate for a more cautious approach—incremental adoption coupled with a continued reliance on fossil fuels. Yet, this half-hearted strategy is akin to treading water in a rising tide. Others propose synthetic biofuels, a compromise between the organic and the manufactured. While these alternatives are worth exploring, they cannot be our sole focus. The true solution is a harmonious blend of natural and technological evolution.

The road ahead is not without its bumps and bends. It requires a paradigm shift, a reimagining of what is possible. As we venture forth, let us carry with us the lessons of the past, the ingenuity of the present, and the dreams of the future.

We stand upon the precipice of change. Will we take the leap and soar on the winds of sustainable growth, or will we retreat to the familiar but barren plains of fossil fuels? The choice is ours, the time is now. Together, let us forge a path where automobiles no longer leave a trail of smog but a legacy of balance with nature. For in this vision, oil does not merely function but flourishes, and we do not merely survive; we thrive. This is where God becomes even more glorified.

Further Reading

Anton Alexandru Kiss .
   Process Intensification Technologies for Biodiesel Production: Reactive Separation Processes

(SpringerBriefs in Applied Sciences and Technology). 2014

Balakrishna R. Geetha, Sakar Mohan, et al. Developments in Biodiesel: Feedstock, Production, and Properties: Volume 84 (Green Chemistry Series)

Barclay V. Martí, Simon P. Neill
Opportunities in Bio-Based Building Blocks for Thermoplastic Polymers
Reference Module in Materials Science and Materials Engineering, 2016

Ephraim E. Enabor, Professor. *Industrial Utilisation of Natural Rubber (Hevea braziliensis) Seed, Latex and Wood.* Published by Rubber Research Institute of Nigeria, 1986.

Esslinger, Hartmut.
A fine line: How Design Strategies are Shaping the Future of Business - 1st Edition, 2009.

Fuessl A., A. Schneller
Biodiesel Production and Technologies
Encyclopedia of Sustainable Technologies, 2017, pp. 261-272

Gorton, A.D.T. "The Influence of the Polymer on the Properties of Foam Backing for Carpets - A.D.T. Gorton, 1975." *SAGE Journals*, journals.sagepub.com/doi/abs/10.1177/15280 8377500400403.

Meisam Tabatabaei and Mortaza AghbashloBiodiesel: From Production to Combustion (Biofuel and Biorefinery Technologies Book 8)

Norul M. Sidek, Mohamad R. Othman
Sustainable Biodiesel Production
Encyclopedia of Renewable and Sustainable Materials, Volume 2, 2020, pp. 347-355

Okonkwo Chinwe P and Modestus O Okwu. Feedstocks for Sustainable Biodiesel Production: Characterization, Selection, and Optimization. 2024

Phillip Westinghouse, Alan Adrian Delfin Cota, et al. Introduction to Biodiesel Production, 1st Edition: How to Create Your Own Batches and a Waste Oil Processor at Home.

Rockson Rapu

Waking Up The Troubled Giant: Industry Captains Sharing Intimate Stories About Their Nigeria of Yesterday. 2021

Shangeetha Ganesan, Hao Sen Siow, Akintomiwa O. Esan, Sivajothi Nadarajah, Nur Liyana Abdul Manaff . Production of Biodiesel from Non-Edible Sources

Syed H. Shah
    Ocean (Marine) Energy
    Comprehensive Energy Systems, Volume 1, 2018, pp. 733-769

Techno-economic Analysis of Heat Pumping Technology for Oleochemical Fatty Acid Fractionation
Computer Aided Chemical Engineering, Volume 48, 2020, pp. 1075-1080

William Kemp. Biodiesel Basics and Beyond: A Comprehensive Guide to Production and Use for the Home and Farm - 2015

Yuanrui Sang, David Souders
    Ocean Renewable Energy Test Centers
    Comprehensive Renewable Energy, Volume 8, 2022, pp. 123-148

ABOUT THE AUTHOR

Rockson Rapu is a British polymer scientist and business consultant, born into a family of men and women of God from Nigeria. After his Master's degree in Business Administration from The University of Hull, he was called into business, and the gracious Hand of the Lord Almighty was upon his life and led him to excel as an entrepreneur and mentor to the next generation. He is the award winning author of – SAVING HER FROM JEZEBEL, SAVING HIM FROM ABSALOM, and WAKING UP THE TROUBLED GIANT.

Rockson Rapu is married and blessed with three diligent daughters and many spiritual sons and daughters, by whom he has been inspired to share so much business secrets through his books.

Printed in Great Britain
by Amazon